Cambridge English

OFFICIAL

SECOND EDITION

First
TRAINER

SIX PRACTICE TESTS WITHOUT ANSWERS

Peter May

Cambridge University Press
www.cambridge.org/elt

Cambridge English Language Assessment
www.cambridgeenglish.org

Information on this title: www.cambridge.org/firsttrainer

First edition © Cambridge University Press 2012
Second edition © Cambridge University Press and UCLES 2015

First published 2012
Second edition 2015
Reprinted 2015

Printed in Dubai by Oriental Press

A catalogue record for this publication is available from the British Library

ISBN 978-1-107-47017-0 Six Practice Tests without answers with Audio
ISBN 978-1-107-47018-7 Six Practice Tests with answers with Audio
ISBN 978-1-107-47021-7 Audio CDs (3)

Additional resources for this publication at www.cambridge.org/firsttrainer

Contents

Introduction   Second edition

Who is *First Trainer* for?

This book is suitable for anyone who is preparing to take the Cambridge English: First (FCE). You can use *First Trainer* in class with your teacher, or – in the case of the with-answers edition of the book – on your own at home.

What is *First Trainer*?

First Trainer contains six practice tests for Cambridge English: First, each covering the Reading and Use of English, Writing, Listening and Speaking papers. Guided Tests 1 and 2 consist of both training and practice for the exam, while Tests 3–6 are entirely practice. All six tests are at exam level and are of First standard.

Test 1 contains information about each part of each paper, plus step-by-step guidance to take you through each kind of First task type, with examples and tips clearly linked to the questions. In the Reading and Use of English, Writing and Speaking papers, it also presents and practises grammar, vocabulary and functional language directly relevant to particular task types. This is supported by work on correcting common grammar mistakes made by First candidates in the exam as shown by the **Cambridge Learner Corpus**. For more information on the Cambridge Learner Corpus see page 6. In Writing, you work with extracts from actual candidate scripts from the Corpus, and in Speaking you listen to sample recordings of each part of the paper. The **Explanatory answer key** tells you which answers are correct and why, and explains why other possible answers are wrong.

Test 2 also contains training for the exam, in addition to revision from Test 1. Here too there is language input, as well as some step-by-step guidance to task types with further examples, advice and tips. In Writing, there is a full focus on the task types not covered in Test 1.

Tests 3–6 contain a wide range of topics, text types and exam items, enabling you to practise the skills you have developed and the language you have learnt in Tests 1 and 2.

How to use *First Trainer*

Test 1 Training

- For each part of each paper you should begin by studying **Task information**, which tells you the facts you need to know, such as what the task type tests and the kinds of questions it uses.

- Throughout Test 1, you will see information marked **Tip!** These tips give you practical advice on how to tackle each task type.

- In all papers, training exercises help you develop the skills you need, e.g. reading for gist, by working through example items of a particular task type.

- For parts 1-4 of **Reading and Use of English**, both parts of **Writing** and all parts of **Speaking**, **Useful language** presents and practises grammatical structures, vocabulary or functional expressions that are often tested by particular task types.

- Many exercises involve focusing on and correcting common language mistakes made by actual First candidates, as shown by the **Cambridge Learner Corpus** (see page 6).

- In **Listening**, you are prompted to use one of the numbered CDs, e.g. ⟨1 02⟩. If you are working on your own using the with-answers edition of *First Trainer*, you will need a CD player (or a computer if you are using the downloadable MP3 files). Note that the numbers on these files are the same as the CD.

- In **Writing**, Test 1 covers Part 1 (essay), as well as the email, article and report tasks in Part 2. You study **sample answers** from the **Cambridge Learner Corpus** written by actual First candidates in the exam, as well as model answers to help you perfect your skills. The **Explanatory answer key** contains answers to the exercises, plus more model texts. You finish each part by writing your own text, bringing in what you have learnt in **Useful language**.

- In **Speaking**, you are prompted to use one of the numbered Mp3 files or CDs, e.g. ⟨1 10⟩, and do written tasks while you listen to examples of each part of the paper. You can practise speaking on your own or with a partner, using what you have learnt in **Useful language**.

- In all papers, **Action plan** gives you clear step-by-step guidance on how to approach each task type.

- You then work through an exam-style task, often doing exercises based on the guidance in **Action plan** and then following the exam instructions. As you do so, **Advice** boxes suggest ways of dealing with particular exam items.

- Answers to all items are in the **Explanatory answer key**, which explains why the correct answers are right and others are wrong. For **Listening**, the parts of the transcripts which give the correct answers are underlined in the texts.

Test 2 Training

- Test 2 contains many of the same features as Test 1, including exercises that focus on exam instructions, texts and tasks, **Tip!** information, **Advice** boxes for many exam items, **Useful language** and an **Explanatory answer key**.

- There is further work based on mistakes frequently made by First candidates as shown by the **Cambridge Learner Corpus**.

- There is also an emphasis on revision, with cross-references for each task type to the relevant **Task information** and **Action plan** in Test 1. You should refer back to these before you begin working through each part.

- Test 2 **Writing** covers Part 1 (essay) plus the letter, review and article tasks in Part 2, also with sample answers and authentic candidates' texts from the **Cambridge Learner Corpus**.

- You should try to do the exam tasks under exam conditions where possible.

Tests 3–6 Exam practice

- In Tests 3, 4, 5 and 6, you can apply the skills and language you have learnt in guided Tests 1 and 2.

- You can do these tests and the four papers within them in any order, but you should always try to keep to the time recommended for each paper. For the Listening paper, you must **listen to each recording twice only**.

- It will be easier to keep to the exam instructions if you can find somewhere quiet to work, and ensure there are no interruptions.

- For the Speaking paper it is better if you can work with a partner, but if not, you can follow the instructions and do all four parts on your own.

- If you have the with-answers edition of the book, you can check your answers for yourself, and also study the Listening transcripts after you have completed the tasks.

The Cambridge Learner Corpus (CLC)

The Cambridge Learner Corpus (CLC) is a large collection of exam scripts written by candidates taking Cambridge ESOL English exams around the world. It currently contains over 90,000 scripts and is growing all the time. It forms part of the Cambridge International Corpus (CIC) and it has been built up by Cambridge University Press and Cambridge ESOL. The CLC currently contains scripts from over:

- 90,000 students
- 100 different first languages
- 180 different countries

Exercises and extracts from candidates' answers from Writing in *First Trainer* which are based on the CLC are indicated by this icon:  Find out about the Cambridge Learner Corpus at www.cambridge.org/corpus.

Other features of *First Trainer*

- Full-colour **visual material** for the Speaking paper of all six tests in the Speaking appendix.
- For Tests 1 and 2, the **Explanatory answer key** in the with-answers edition on pages 183–234 tells you which answers are correct, and why. In some cases, such as multiple-choice questions, it also explains why the other options are wrong.
- In the **with-answers** edition, you can check your answers to Tests 3–6 in the key at the back. In the case of Listening, the parts of the transcript that give the correct answers are underlined.
- **Photocopiable answer sheets** for the Reading and Use of English and Listening papers are at the back of the book. Before you take the exam, you should study these so that you know how to mark or write your answers correctly. In Writing, the question paper has plenty of lined space for you to write your answers.
- **Three audio CDs also available as downloadable MP3 files** containing recordings for the Listening papers of the six First tests plus recordings of different parts of the Speaking test to serve as samples. The listening material is indicated by a different icon in *First Trainer* for each of the CDs:

The Cambridge English: First examination

Level of the Cambridge English: First examination

First is at level B2 on the Common European Framework (CEF). When you reach this level, these are some of the things you should be able to do:

- You can scan written texts for the information you need, and understand detailed instructions or advice.
- You can understand or give a talk on a familiar subject, and keep a conversation going on quite a wide range of subjects.
- You can make notes while someone is talking, and write a letter that includes different kinds of requests.

Grading

- The overall First grade that you receive is based on the total score you achieve in all four papers.
- The Reading and Use of English paper carries 40% of the possible marks, while each of Writing, Listening and Speaking carry 20% of the possible marks.
- There is no minimum score for each paper, so you don't have to 'pass' all four in order to pass the exam.
- You receive a certificate if you pass the exam with grade A (the highest grade), B or C. Grades D and E are fails.
- Whatever your grade, you will receive a Statement of Results. This includes a graphical profile of how well you did in each paper and shows your relative performance in each one.
- For more information on grading and results, go to the Cambridge English Language Assessment website (see 'Further information' on page 9).

Content of the Cambridge English: First examination

The Cambridge English: First examination has four papers, each consisting of a number of parts. For details on each part, see the page reference under the *Task information* heading in these tables.

Reading and Use of English 1 hour 15 minutes

Parts 1 and 3 mainly test your vocabulary; Part 2 mainly tests your grammar. Part 4 often tests both. There is one mark for each correct answer in Parts 1, 2 and 3, but two marks for a correct answer in Part 4. You can write on the question paper, but you must remember to transfer your answers to the separate answer sheet before the end of the test.

Texts in Part 5 are 550–650 words each, while those in Parts 6 and 7 are 500–600 words each. They are taken from newspaper and magazine articles, fiction, reports, advertisements, correspondence, messages and informational material such as brochures, guides or manuals. There are two marks for each correct answer in Parts 5 and 6; there is one mark for every correct answer in Part 7.

Part	Task type	No. of questions	Format	Task information
1	multiple choice gap-fill	8	You choose from words A, B, C or D to fill in each gap in a text.	page 10
2	open gap-fill	8	You think of a word to fill in each of the gaps in a text.	page 14
3	word formation	8	You think of the correct form of a given word to fill in each gap in a text.	page 17
4	key word transformations	6	You have to complete a sentence with a given word so that it means the same as another sentence.	page 20
5	multiple choice	6	You read a text followed by questions with four options: A, B, C or D.	page 24
6	gapped text	6	You read a text with sentences removed, then fill in the gaps by choosing sentences from a jumbled list.	page 28
7	multiple matching	10	You read one or more texts and match the relevant sections to what the questions say.	page 31

Writing 1 hour 20 minutes

You have to do Part 1 (question 1) plus any **one** of the Part 2 tasks. In Part 2 you can choose one of questions 2–4. The possible marks for Part 1 and Part 2 are the same. In all tasks you are told who you are writing to and why.

Part	Task type	No. of words	Format	Task information
1	Question 1: essay	140–190	You give your opinion on a topic using the two ideas given plus an idea of your own.	page 34
2	Questions 2–4 possible tasks: email/ letter, article, report or review	140–190	You do a task based on a situation.	pages 38, 43, 47

Listening about 40 minutes

You will both hear and see the instructions for each task, and you will hear each of the four parts twice. You will hear pauses announced, and you can use this time to look at the task and the questions. At the end of the test you will have five minutes to copy your answers onto the answer sheet.

If one person is speaking, you may hear information, news, instructions, a commentary, a documentary, a lecture, a message, a public announcement, a report, a speech, a talk or an advertisement. If two people are talking, you might hear a conversation, a discussion, an interview, part of a radio play, etc.

Part	Task type	No. of questions	Format	Task information
1	multiple choice	8	You hear one or two people talking for about 30 seconds in eight different situations. For each question, you choose from answers A, B or C.	page 50
2	sentence completion	10	You hear one person talking for about three minutes. For each question, you complete sentences by writing a word or short phrase.	page 53
3	multiple matching	5	You hear five different extracts, of about 30 seconds each, with a common theme. For each one you choose from a list of eight possible answers.	page 55
4	multiple choice	7	You hear one or two people talking for about three minutes. For each question, you choose from answers A, B or C.	page 57

Speaking 14 minutes

You will probably do the Speaking test with one other candidate, though sometimes it is necessary to form groups of three. There will be two examiners, but one of them does not take part in the conversation. The examiner will indicate who you should talk to in each part of the test.

Part	Task type	Minutes	Format	Task information
1	The examiner asks you some questions.	2	You talk about yourself.	page 59
2	You talk on your own.	4	You talk about two pictures and then comment on the other candidate's pictures.	page 61
3	You talk to the other candidate.	4	You discuss some diagrams or pictures together.	page 64
4	You talk about things connected with the topic of Part 3.	4	You take part in a discussion with both the other candidate and the examiner.	page 66

Further information

The information about Cambridge English: First contained in *First Trainer* is designed to be an overview of the exam. For a full description of the First examination, including information about task types, testing focus and preparation for the exam, please see the Cambridge English: First Handbook, which can be obtained from the Cambridge English Language Assessment website or from the address below.

Cambridge English Language Assessment

1 Hills Road

Cambridge CB1 2EU

United Kingdom

Task information

- In Part 1 you choose from words **A**, **B**, **C** or **D** to fill in each gap in a text. Options **A**, **B**, **C** and **D** are always the same kind of word (e.g. *verbs*).

- Part 1 mainly tests vocabulary but you may also need to understand grammatical links between words, or the text as a whole.

- Words that often go together, called 'collocations', are frequently tested and so are words followed by a preposition (e.g. *aware of*).

Useful language: collocations

1 Match each noun in the box with the verbs below. (Some nouns go with more than one verb.) Then think of more nouns to add to each column.

a break	a job	~~a mistake~~	a noise	a party	a photo	a shower
friends	fun	notes	progress	riding	shopping	skiing
some homework	sports	swimming	the bus	the dishes	time	

Tip! Prepare for this task by keeping a record of words that often go together (e.g. *ride a bike, loud noise*).

make	have	go	take	do
a mistake				

2 Note down as many nouns as you can that often go with each of these verbs.

| beat | catch | earn | hold | keep | lose | miss | pass | play | save | spend | win |

3 Correct one mistake in sentences 1–10 written by First candidates, using verbs from Exercises 1 and 2.

1 We could go to the cinema and we could also make shopping.
2 It's a great honour for our company to earn a prize like this.
3 The other students are interesting and I think I'll spend a nice time with them.
4 I would like to travel during the school holidays, in order not to lose any classes.
5 I hope you will pass a good time at the wedding next month.
6 You can catch a taxi to come to our office.
7 I enjoyed watching a match on TV. The team in blue won the team in yellow.
8 We would be pleased to make business with your company.
9 In modern society, cars take a large part in our lives.
10 The old person next door lives all alone. Please have an eye on her while I am away.

4 Write each of these adjectives and verbs on the correct line or lines. Then think of more words for each line.

afraid	agree	~~apply~~	aware	belong	bound
~~care~~	depend	familiar	~~famous~~	interested	involved
jealous	keen	object	pleased	rely	succeed

1 .....apply, care, famous.......... for   4 .... in
2 .... of   5 .... to
3 .... on   6 .... with

5 For each of sentences 1–10, choose the correct word, A, B, C or D.

1 The office manager doesn't … of staff wearing jeans to work.
  A admire   B approve   C respect   D appreciate
2 Witnesses say the lorry driver was … for the accident.
  A likely   B guilty   C responsible   D probable
3 The Australian city of Sydney is … for its bridge and opera house.
  A proud   B famous   C impressive   D outstanding
4 Sadly, there are always a few who are … of other people's achievements.
  A jealous   B angry   C greedy   D dissatisfied
5 Nathan is an engineer, … in solar energy systems.
  A focusing   B dedicating   C specialising   D concentrating
6 After three attempts, Nigel finally … in passing his driving test.
  A fulfilled   B managed   C achieved   D succeeded
7 Clara's younger sister … on going with her to the party.
  A insisted   B requested   C required   D demanded
8 The events shown in this film are … on a true story.
  A fixed   B based   C set   D rested
9 Isabel isn't a greedy person. She's … with what she already has.
  A positive   B glad   C cheerful   D satisfied
10 A good friend is someone you can always … on to help you.
  A believe   B trust   C rely   D bargain

Action plan

1 Look at the title and the example.

2 Without filling in any gaps, quickly read the text to get an idea of what it's about.

3 For each gap, decide what kind of word (e.g. *nouns*, *adverbs*) the four options are.

4 Study the words either side of the gap, underlining any possible collocations.

5 Try each answer in the gap, checking whether it fits grammatically.

6 Check that the word you choose fits the overall meaning of the sentence.

7 Read through the completed sentence, checking that everything makes sense.

Follow the exam instructions, using the advice to help you.

For questions **1–8**, read the text opposite and decide which answer (**A, B, C** or **D**) best fits each gap. There is an example at the beginning (**0**).

Tip! Write the example answer into gap (0). It will help you understand the beginning of the text.

Tip! If you're not sure of an answer, cross out any you know are wrong and choose from those remaining.

Example:

0 **A** well   **B** much   **C** lots   **D** far

| 0 | A | B | C | D |

| | | | | |

1 **A** along   **B** away   **C** out   **D** beyond

2 **A** referred   **B** known   **C** called   **D** named

3 **A** include   **B** enclose   **C** cover   **D** range

4 **A** high   **B** rapid   **C** light   **D** fast

5 **A** assessed   **B** supposed   **C** estimated   **D** regarded

6 **A** largely   **B** greatly   **C** importantly **D** absolutely

7 **A** arrived   **B** reached   **C** finished   **D** closed

8 **A** caught up with **B** put up with **C** come up with **D** kept up with

Advice

1 Which means 'outside'?

2 Which completes a fixed phrase with 'as'?

3 Look at the two prepositions in this part of the sentence.

4 Only one of these goes with 'speed'.

5 Which has the correct meaning and fits the verb form?

6 Which adverb can go with 'increased'?

7 Which goes with 'agreement' and the preposition 'on'.

8 Which three-part verb means 'think of'?

Space junk

The Space Age began **(0)** .... over half a century ago, and ever since then the area just **(1)** .... the Earth's atmosphere has been filling up with all kinds of man-made objects that have become **(2)** .... as 'space junk'. The items up there **(3)** .... from old satellites and parts of rockets to hundreds of thousands of pieces smaller than one centimetre, all of them travelling at extremely **(4)** .... speed. Over the last five years, the number of such objects in space is **(5)** .... to have risen by 50 per cent, and this has **(6)** .... increased the risk of damage to working satellites or space vehicles with crews on board.

International agreement has therefore now been **(7)** .... on limiting the amount of new space junk. Scientists have also **(8)** .... some interesting suggestions for tidying up space. These include using laser beams, giant nets and even an enormous umbrella-like device to collect tiny bits of junk.

Tip! Fill in your answers on the question paper in pencil. This will help you check the completed text when you finish.

Task information

- In Part 2 there is a text with eight gaps. There are no sets of words from which to choose.
- Part 2 mainly tests 'grammar words' like articles (e.g. *the, an*), auxiliary verbs (e.g. *will, has*), pronouns (e.g. *they, who*), prepositions (e.g. *on, during*), linking expressions (e.g. *despite*) and verb forms (e.g. *would do*), as well as words in phrasal verbs (e.g. *set off*) and fixed phrases (e.g. *in favour of*).
- You must only use one word in each gap and your spelling must be correct.

Useful language: relative pronouns and linking expressions

1 Questions in Part 2 sometimes focus on relative pronouns like *which*.
Complete these rules with the words in the box.

> that (x3)   when   where   which   who   whose

> **Rules**
>
> In any kind of relative clause, we can use **(1)** .... for people, **(2)** .... for things, **(3)** .... for possession, **(4)** .... for time and **(5)** .... for places. In a defining relative clause, we can also use **(6)** .... for people or things, e.g. *the girl* **(7)** .... *sang really well*; *the tree* **(8)** .... *grew so tall*.

2 Tick ✓ the sentences which are correct and replace the relative pronoun in those that are wrong. Sometimes more than one answer is possible.

1 Do you remember Simon, whose used to teach us?
2 I think that the best time to come is in early August, which we have the celebrations.
3 They invited me to a pop concert which took place in Rio last month.
4 I'm writing in reply to the advertisement who asks for people to help in a summer camp.
5 I met some people there which became my good friends.
6 It was a period of my life that I had many problems.
7 It was not until I was seventeen that I started writing down all what happened to me every day.
8 Instead of going to a nursery, I went to a school which children learnt by playing.
9 There are some people whose aim in life is to earn as much money as possible.
10 The Park Hotel, that I found in the guide, is now closed so I stayed at the Central.

3 Complete the text using relative pronouns.

Melanie Johnson, **(1)** .... house is opposite mine, is my favourite neighbour. She's a warm and friendly person **(2)** .... always likes to help other people. In the afternoon, **(3)** .... I come home, she often waves and smiles to me from her front garden, **(4)** .... she spends a lot of time in spring and summer. It has some lovely flowers, **(5)** .... she planted herself, and last week she gave some to my mother, **(6)** .... birthday was on Friday. She's always been generous like that. I remember years ago, **(7)** .... I was about ten, she painted a picture for me **(8)** .... was so lovely that I put it on my bedroom wall. It's still there.

Tip! You always have to fill in the gap in Part 2. The missing word can never be left out of the sentence.

4 Some questions in Part 2 test linking expressions like *although* or *unless*.
Put the words and expressions in the box under the correct heading below.

although	~~and~~	as long as	as well as	~~because~~	because of
besides	~~but~~	however	if	in addition to	in case
even so	even though	in spite of	due to (the	owing to	provided (that)
in order that	in order to	so	fact that)	~~to~~	unless
so as to	since	despite (the	on account of	(and) yet	
whereas	while	fact that)	though		

addition	conditional	contrast	purpose	reason
and	if	but	to	because

5 In these sentences written by First candidates, circle the correct alternative in *italics*.

1 The boat trip along the river was cancelled *because / because of* the bad weather.
2 We will have to consider joining another club *unless / besides* you make the improvements.
3 I am enclosing a telephone card *in case / if* your mobile phone doesn't work in Italy.
4 The visit should be longer *so/so as* to give people the chance to see the whole city.
5 The dates of the exam need to change *in order / in order that* all students can take it.
6 We had to move out of the city centre *owing to / because* the rise in prices.
7 *Even though / Even so* we are irritated by commercials, they can give us useful information.
8 We must replace the loudspeakers *as long as / since* the current ones aren't satisfactory.
9 You can ask the teacher for help *if / in case* you need further guidance.
10 *Although / In spite of* the fact the accommodation is cheap, it is very comfortable.

6 Complete the text with words from Exercise 4. Sometimes more than one answer is possible.

It was getting late by the time Sam and Marco approached the summit, on **(1)** ..*account*.. of the terrible weather on their way up. In **(2)** .... to high winds that nearly swept them right off the mountain, they faced freezing temperatures and heavy snowfalls. And **(3)** .... neither of them had any thoughts of giving up. In **(4)** .... of the awful conditions they were determined to keep climbing even **(5)** .... every step was now a huge effort, **(6)** .... to the fact they were so high up and the air was so thin. As **(7)** .... as that, Marco was feeling quite ill, probably **(8)** .... of the height and a lack of food. But they knew that **(9)** .... reach the top they couldn't stop for anything, even meals. They also knew that **(10)** .... they got there this time, they would probably never have another chance to try. And Sam was sure that as **(11)** .... as they could begin going down by three o'clock, they would make it safely back to base camp that night – **(12)** .... they would both be very, very tired.

> **Tip!** Answers are never hyphenated words such as *long-term*.

Action plan

1 Look at the title and the example.
2 Without trying to fill in any answers, quickly read the text to see what it's about.
3 For each gap, look at the context and decide what kind of word (e.g. *relative pronoun*) is needed.
4 Study the words either side of the gap for more clues.
5 Think of words that might fit and try each one.
6 When you have filled in all the gaps, read your text to check it makes sense.

1 Quickly read the text. Which paragraph is about attitudes to chewing gum? Which is about the history of chewing gum?

2 Follow the exam instructions, using the advice to help you.

Tip! Gaps may have more than one possible answer, but you must only write one.

Tip! If you can't answer a particular question, go on to the others and come back to it later when you have completed more of the text.

For questions **9–16**, read the text below and think of the word which best fits each gap. Use only one word in each gap. There is an example at the beginning (**0**).

Example: | 0 | T | O | | | | | | | | | | | | | | | | |

Chewing gum

We still tend (**0**) .... think chewing gum is a fairly recent invention, even (**9**) .... there is evidence it was used 5,000 years ago in Finland. The Ancient Greeks also chewed gum, as (**10**) .... the Aztecs in Mexico during the sixteenth century. As far as we know, however, it wasn't (**11**) .... 1869 that chewing gum became popular in its present form, (**12**) .... a New York inventor called Thomas Adams first had the idea of adding flavour to it.

Nowadays, of course, it is chewed around the world, (**13**) .... the fact that it continues to be regarded by some (**14**) .... an unpleasant habit. Unfortunately, far too many people drop used gum onto the pavement, (**15**) .... it remains for some time because it is extremely difficult to remove once it has stuck to the surface. On the other hand, those (**16**) .... favour of chewing gum claim it helps them relax, improves their concentration, and helps keep their teeth clean.

Advice

9 You need a word that completes a contrast link.

10 Find a way to avoid repeating the verb.

11 Think of a suitable time link.

12 Which relative pronoun is used for time?

13 Think of a word that completes a contrast link.

14 Which preposition often follows 'regarded'?

15 Which relative pronoun is used for a place?

16 Think of a preposition that goes with 'favour of'.

Tip! Never write contracted forms like *she's* or *wouldn't* as they count as **two** words.

Task information

- In Part 3 you read a text containing eight gaps. At the end of some lines there is a word in capital letters for you to form one appropriate word to fill each gap.
- Part 3 mainly tests your ability to form new words and different parts of speech.
- You may, for example, need to form adverbs by adding *-ly* to adjectives, make nouns plural by adding *-s* or *-es*, change verb/adjective forms by adding *-ed* or *-ing*, or form comparative/superlative forms by adding *-er* or *-est*.
- You may also have to make spelling changes (e.g. *long* to *length*). You must always get the spelling correct to get a point!

Useful language: word formation

1   To do Part 3 successfully, you need to know which affixes are often used for different parts of speech. Match the prefixes and suffixes a–d with 1–4. Write an example for each.

> **Tip!** Keep a record of words with affixes that you see while you are reading in English.

a   un- in- im- dis- ir-

1   people who do jobs – bus driv**er**, employ**ee**, art**ist**, shop assist**ant**, instruct**or**

b   -er -ee -ist -ant -or

2   negative prefixes (mainly used for adjectives but also some verbs and nouns)

c   -tion -ment -ness -ity -ance -ence -ship

3   adjective suffixes

d   -ful -less -able -ous -ive -itive -y -ible

4   noun suffixes

2a   Complete the table, using your dictionary if you need to. Use affixes from Exercise 1 and follow these spelling rules:

- For adjectives ending in *-y*, change the *y* to an *i* (e.g. *easy/easily*).
- With suffixes beginning with a vowel, drop the final *e* (e.g. *prepare/preparation*).
- For some words, you need to make other spelling changes (e.g. *high/height*, *freeze/frozen*, *little/least*).

verb	noun(s)	adjective(s)	adverb(s)
comfort	comfort(s), discomfort(s)	(un)comfortable	(un)comfortably
employ			
hope			
	noise(s), noisiness		
lose			
	science(s), scientist(s)		
relate			
succeed			

> **Tip!** When you learn a word, use a good dictionary to find out which affixes you can add and how these change the meaning. Note these down, with example sentences.

b   Where more than one word is possible, explain the difference, e.g. comfort – *pleasant*, discomfort – *unpleasant*.

3 Complete the sentences using the word in capitals. Use words from the table in Exercise 2.

1 Our neighbours are friendly so we have a good ...relationship... with them. **RELATION**

2 Most .... agree that sea levels will continue to rise in the coming years. **SCIENCE**

3 The huge waterfall was so .... that I couldn't hear a word anyone said. **NOISE**

4 In an area of such high .... , we must provide new jobs for local people. **EMPLOY**

5 Our situation on the island seemed .... as we had no water or food left. **HOPE**

6 The 800-kilometre journey in an old bus with hard seats was very .... **COMFORT**

7 Our plan to save the trees was .... and sadly they have all now been cut down. **SUCCESS**

8 The .... of so much rainforest will have a terrible effect on the climate. **LOSE**

4 These sentences written by First candidates each contain word formation errors. Correct the mistakes. Which of 1–10:

- use the wrong affix?
- have a spelling mistake?
- confuse singular and plural?

1 The paramedics gave him first aid and, without *loosing* a second, put him in the ambulance.

2 More and more people in my country are out of work and *unemployments* is getting worse.

3 I think the fact that only 60 per cent of the money will go to the hospital is *inacceptable*.

4 The gang must have been very careful, because the police could find no *evidences* at all.

5 You can develop a good *relation* with your pet over time.

6 They work with *scientifict* institutions to study the environment in the area.

7 I think that this is a good way to solve the *disagree* between Pat and his friend.

8 I am *hopefull* that I will be able to do this job in the future.

9 I had to work for 100 hours a week and ate at *unregularly* times.

10 *Employeers* should provide insurance for all of their staff.

Advice

1 The article 'a' and the adjective 'good' mean we need a noun. If people are 'friendly' we probably get on well with them, so we have 'a good relation**ship**'.

2 The verb 'agree' needs a subject, probably a kind of people. It is plural so this noun must be plural, too.

3 The missing word describes 'waterfall' so it's an adjective. If the person 'couldn't hear' it means there was a lot of noise.

4 After the adjective 'high' we need a noun from 'employ'. If 'new jobs' are required, there can't be enough now, so the meaning will be negative.

5 The missing word describes 'situation' so it must be an adjective. That situation was clearly negative.

6 We need an adjective to describe the 'journey'. We must make 'comfort' negative by adding both a suffix and a negative prefix.

7 The word 'sadly' shows it is a negative idea, so we need an adjective to describe 'plan' with a negative prefix.

8 After the article 'the' we need a noun meaning something lost, but we need to be careful with the spelling.

Action plan

1 Quickly read the title and the text. What's it about?

2 Look at each word in CAPITALS and the words before and after the gap. Is the missing word likely to be a noun, a verb, or another part of speech?

3 If it's a noun, is it countable or uncountable?

4 If it's an adjective, is it positive or negative?

5 Does the word in CAPITALS need more than one change?

6 Check the word you have chosen fits the context and is spelt correctly.

1 Look at the example (0). What kind of word comes after *the*?
What suffix must you add to *embarrass* to form this kind of word?

2 Follow the exam instructions, using the advice to help you.

For questions **17–24**, read the text below. Use the word given in capitals at the end of some of the lines to form a word that fits in the gap in the same line. There is an example at the beginning (0).

Write your answers IN CAPITAL LETTERS on the separate answer sheet.

Example: **0**   E M B A R R A S S M E N T

Remembering people's names

Most of us have suffered the **(0)** .... of forgetting someone's   **EMBARRASS**

name. Often we fail to pay attention when **(17)** .... are   **INTRODUCE**

made, but later on in the conversation we don't want to appear

(18) .... by asking them what they're called.   **POLITE**

Fortunately, there are some simple ways you can **(19)** ....   **COME**

this problem. One is to improve your powers of **(20)** ....   **OBSERVE**

Practise studying faces in public places, making a mental note

of physical **(21)** .... such as high foreheads or narrow   **CHARACTER**

eyebrows. You'll be surprised what a wide **(22)** .... of shapes   **VARY**

and sizes people's features have. Then, when you first meet someone,

remember them as 'Laura with the small nose', for example.

With surnames, make **(23)** .... associations. For instance,   **VISION**

imagine people called Cook, Ford or King making a meal, driving a

car or wearing a crown, respectively. Finally, ending with the person's

name, as in 'See you later, Max.' is a good way of **(24)** ....   **SURE**

that you don't forget it.

Advice

17 Be careful with the 'e'.

18 Does the missing word have a positive or negative meaning?

19 Think of a compound word that means 'solve' here.

20 Take care with the final 'e'.

21 Is a singular or plural word needed?

22 What needs to happen to the 'y'?

23 You need to change three letters.

24 Which verb form is needed after 'of'?

Tip! Remember you always have to change the word given, and that sometimes you will need a prefix *and* a suffix.

3 For each of the words in capitals in the exam task, find other words from it and keep a record, with example sentences.

Task information

- In Part 4 there are six questions – each with a lead-in sentence, a key word, and a second gapped sentence for you to complete.

- Part 4 tests grammar *and* vocabulary by asking you to use different structures and words to express the same idea.

- You have to write your answer in two, three, four or five words. This includes the word in capitals, which you have to use and mustn't change. You lose marks if you ignore any of these instructions.

- Each correct answer gets two marks, with one mark for each part of the answer. So Part 4 has more possible marks than Parts 1, 2 or 3.

Useful language: key word transformations

1 Part 4 sometimes focuses on expressions followed by the *-ing* form or *to* + infinitive. Study the rules and add the words in the box to the lists in 1–3. Then add three more examples to each.

after	avoid	carry on	decide	despite	easy
enjoy	expect	forget	give up	help someone	
it's no use	it's not worth	likely	plan	pleased	put off
stop	suggest	tell someone	there's no point (in)	try	
want something	without				

Rules

1 We use the *-ing* form after
- some verbs (e.g. *It **keeps** rain**ing***)
Examples: ....
- prepositions (e.g. *I'm **keen on** rid**ing***)
Examples: ....
- two-part (and three-part) verbs (e.g. *I'm **looking forward to** meet**ing** her*)
Examples: ....
- some expressions (e.g. *I'm **fed up with** wait**ing***)
Examples: ....

2 We use the *to* + infinitive form after
- some verbs (e.g. *I **want to leave***)
Examples: ....
- some verbs + object (e.g. *He **asked me to go***)
Examples: ....
- some adjectives (e.g. *I was **glad to** see her*)
Examples: ....

3 We can use either *-ing* or *to* + infinitive after some verbs, but with different meanings, e.g. *I **regret to tell** you* (I'm sorry to tell you this), or *I **regret** tell**ing** you* (I'm sorry I told you).
Examples: ....

2 Complete the second sentence so that it means the same as the first sentence, using the *-ing* or the *to* + infinitive form of the verb.

1 I'm going out this evening.   I've decided *to go out this evening.*...........
2 I like to listen to music in the evening.   I enjoy ....
3 The bus will probably be late again.   The bus is likely ....
4 We can't play tennis until Saturday.   We'll have to put off ....
5 It doesn't make sense to stay here.   There's no point in ....
6 Although I felt ill, I went to school.   Despite ....
7 I'll be glad if Mark comes to my party.   I want Mark ....
8 Kate didn't remember to call Emma.   Kate forgot ....

3 (⊙) Correct these sentences written by First candidates.

1 To save one dollar a day I gave up to have a coffee in my break time.
2 That is all for now. Don't forget writing soon!
3 We stopped to place orders with your company because deliveries were too often delayed.
4 I'm very glad hearing from you, I really miss you.
5 I will carry on to use my bicycle whenever it is possible.
6 There is no point to open a store in a village when most of the population are working in town during the opening hours.
7 My best friend and I plan seeing a film at the cinema this evening.
8 She suggested to light a fire so we could burn the documents.
9 I regret telling you that we will be forced to put this matter in the hands of our solicitors.
10 I remembered to have seen the escalator on my left when I first went into my room at the hotel.

4 Part 4 questions sometimes test past forms of modal verbs: modal + *have* + past participle (e.g. *There's no reply – she must have left already*). Make a list of other past modal forms and their negatives (e.g. *would have left/would not (wouldn't) have left*).

5 Use past modal forms to complete the second sentence so that it means the same as the first.

1 It's a pity you didn't arrive earlier.   You should *have arrived* .... earlier.
2 I'm sure Jack was happy when he saw his exam results.   Jack must .... happy when he saw his exam results.
3 It's possible that Zoe's friends didn't tell her.   Zoe's friends may .... her.
4 There's just a chance that Sean got you a ticket.   Sean might .... you a ticket.
5 I'm sure your parents weren't pleased when they saw the bill.   Your parents can't .... pleased when they saw the bill.
6 There was no need for you to get up early – go back to bed!   You needn't .... early – go back to bed!
7 Unfortunately, you sent in your application two days late.   You should .... your application two days late.
8 I'm sorry you didn't tell me about this before.   You ought .... me about this before.

6 In these sentences written by First candidates, circle the correct alternative in *italics*.

1 My holiday *should have beginning / should have begun* at midday last Saturday.
2 I saw that somebody had opened the back door, but I didn't have any idea who it *might have been / might had been*.
3 The time that the show *should start / should have started* was 19.30 but it started 45 minutes later.
4 It was really wonderful and I *could have never / could never have* dreamt it would be so good.
5 We *had not to / did not have to* pay for any accommodation there because a friend of Juan put us up.
6 Animals in zoos were not born where they *should have been / must have been* born: in their natural environment.
7 We *didn't need to / needn't to go to* the supermarket when we arrived at the apartment because there was already food there.
8 I *can't have / couldn't have* imagined until that day how difficult it is to live without electrical energy.

Action plan

1 Read the instructions and the example. This will remind you exactly what you have to do.

2 For each question, study both sentences and the key word in CAPITALS. What differences are there between the two sentences?

3 Decide what kind of word (e.g. *noun*) the key word is, and what often follows it (e.g. *preposition*).

4 Begin by thinking about what the question is testing (e.g. *conditionals* or *phrasal verbs*).

5 Think about whether you need to make a grammatical change (e.g. from active to passive) or a vocabulary change (e.g. change *escape* to the phrasal verb *get away*, or change a linking expression like *because* to *on account of*).

6 Check whether you need to make any other changes (e.g. a noun to an adjective, an affirmative to a negative).

7 Check you have included all the information from the first sentence and that you haven't added anything.

Tip! If you can't complete the whole answer, write what you can – you may get one mark.

8 Check that the completed sentence makes sense.

Follow the exam instructions, using the advice to help you.

For questions **25–30**, complete the second sentence so that it has a similar meaning to the first sentence, using the word given. **Do not change the word given**. You must use between **two** and **five** words, including the word given. Here is an example (**0**).

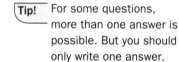

Tip! For some questions, more than one answer is possible. But you should only write one answer.

0 During our holidays, we eat out <u>rather than cook</u> at home.

INSTEAD

During our holidays, we eat out .... at home.

The gap can be filled by the words 'instead of cooking' so you write:

You have to change the underlined words.

Change of verb form needed.

1 mark for 'instead of', 1 mark for 'cooking'.

Example:

0	INSTEAD OF COOKING

Write only the missing words IN CAPITAL LETTERS on the separate answer sheet.

---

25 Thomas spoke so quickly I had difficulty understanding him.

IT

Thomas spoke so quickly I .... him.

26 They've postponed the match and it'll be played next weekend.

PUT

The match .... until next weekend.

27 I'm never going to speak to Louis again.

INTENTION

I've got .... to Louis again.

28 It seems certain that lightning started the forest fire.

HAVE

The forest fire .... by lightning.

29 It wasn't worth going to the market because it was closing.

POINT

The market was closing, so .... going there.

30 We phoned the restaurant, but they said booking a table wasn't necessary.

HAVE

We phoned the restaurant, but they said we .... a table.

Advice

25 What verb often goes before 'it' and an adjective?

26 Phrasal verb needed.

27 Be careful with the form of the second verb.

28 Passive verb form needed.

29 Remember that 'point' is a noun here.

30 Use the negative form of a modal verb.

Tip! Check that your spelling is correct. You will lose marks for spelling mistakes.

Task information

- In Part 5 you read a text followed by six questions with four options: A, B, C or D.
- Questions may test your ability to understand overall meaning, main ideas or details, as well as attitudes or opinions.
- You may need to *infer* meaning (use clues to understand things that aren't actually said).
- The first line can be a question or an unfinished statement.
- Questions follow the order of information in the text.

Reading for gist; dealing with distraction

1   Quickly read the exam instructions and the two paragraphs.

   1   What kind of text is it?

   2   Why did Liam go to the house?

You are going to read an extract from a novel. For questions **31–36**, choose the answer (**A**, **B**, **C** or **D**) which you think fits best according to the text.

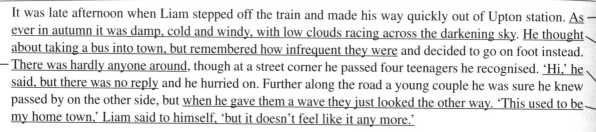

It was late afternoon when Liam stepped off the train and made his way quickly out of Upton station. As ever in autumn it was damp, cold and windy, with low clouds racing across the darkening sky. He thought about taking a bus into town, but remembered how infrequent they were and decided to go on foot instead. There was hardly anyone around, though at a street corner he passed four teenagers he recognised. 'Hi,' he said, but there was no reply and he hurried on. Further along the road a young couple he was sure he knew passed by on the other side, but when he gave them a wave they just looked the other way. 'This used to be my home town,' Liam said to himself, 'but it doesn't feel like it any more.'

Arriving at number 46, he rang the bell and waited. At first nobody came, even though he was right on time and he knew that Carson was expecting him. He rang again, more impatiently. He didn't want to be there a moment longer than necessary. He wondered whether Carson might have changed his mind about helping. Had the plan perhaps become so ambitious that it had scared him off? Eventually, though, the door opened, and a tall, thin, worried-looking man stood there. 'Did you have a good journey? Is everything all right?' Carson asked. 'Yes,' said Liam calmly, 'and if you can give me the package, I'll be on my way.'

2   Look at exam question 31 below: the answer is C. The parts of the text that relate to options A–D are underlined. Write A, B, C or D next to the underlined text and explain why each option is correct or incorrect.

   31   What surprised him about the town?

      A   There were many people on the streets.

      B   The public transport system was poor.

      C   The people he saw were unfriendly.

      D   The weather was rather unpleasant.

3   Look at exam question 32 below: the answer is B. Underline the parts of the text that relate to options A–D and explain why each is correct or incorrect.

   32   How did Liam feel when he was at the house?

      A   pleased he would be able to spend some time there

      B   eager to collect the item and then leave quickly

      C   afraid because he was involved in something big

      D   worried that he might have got there too late

 Tip! Look for clear evidence that the answer you have chosen is correct, and that the other three are incorrect.

Action plan

1 Read the instructions and the title, if there is one. What kind of text (e.g. *magazine article*) is it?

2 Quickly read the text without trying to answer any of the questions. What is it about?

3 Look at the stem of the first question, underlining the key words (i.e. the most important words).

4 Find the relevant part of the text. Draw a vertical line next to it and write down the question number.

5 Read what the text says about the question and try to answer it in your own words.

6 Look at options A, B, C and D. Which is closest to your understanding of what the text says?

7 If you really aren't sure, cross out any options that you think are wrong and then make a guess.

8 Repeat steps 1–7 for each question.

Follow the exam instructions, using the advice to help you.

You are going to read an extract from a novel. For questions **31–36**, choose the answer (**A**, **B**, **C** or **D**) which you think fits best according to the text.

Tip! Questions may ask you to work out the meaning of words or phrases using the context, or to focus on reference words like *it* and *this*.

Tip! Questions could be about the use of examples or comparison, the writer's purpose, or the tone, (e.g. *critical*) of the text.

'Claire, it's Ruth.' Claire held back a sigh and walked into the kitchen to put the coffee machine on. A phone call from her sister was never over quickly.

'Ruth, darling. How are you?' As she waited for her sister to start describing in detail her latest disaster, Claire mulled over how much to reveal about her new business assignment. Her family would have to be told something, of course. Not that they ever came to visit, or called her home phone, or sent her letters. Still, it seemed only right to tell them it meant she was moving out for twelve months. Tuning back into the phone call, Claire realised she had missed some key information and tried to catch up with what her sister was talking about.

'So the doctor said it was probably lack of sleep. You know Sky is a bad sleeper and her nightmares have been worse since she started Year Two.' Claire worked out that someone was unwell, but was unsure whether it was her sister or her six-year-old niece.

Claire thought about her own schooling. Her parents had paid for the best, obviously, although Claire often wondered whether that was to ensure their three children didn't affect their lifestyle, rather than to give their offspring a good start in life. The school had encouraged independence and character but had no time for tears and tantrums. Claire had learned quickly to work hard and stay out of trouble. More than could be said for Ruth. It had been a constant disappointment to her parents that, while their first and third children both achieved academic success, Ruth only acquired a reputation for bad behaviour.

Ruth's next sentence sharply interrupted Claire's thoughts.

'The tests are the week after next. That's why I'm calling. Is there any chance you could come and look after Sky? It's half-term and most of her friends are going skiing. Of course we can't afford that…'

Claire inhaled deeply and forced herself not to rise to the bait. Ruth was always poor and begrudged Claire her success. Claire accepted that looking after a child on your own probably limited your career options, but look at the 'Harry Potter' author J. K. Rowling, it hadn't held her back. She was convinced Ruth could help herself if only she'd try harder. Claire was almost too irritated by the thinly-veiled criticism to react to the request, but not quite.

'Have Sky? How long for? When?' Claire could hear panic in her voice and forced herself to breathe in deeply. Once she was sure she was back in control of her emotions she said in a slow voice, 'I start a new work assignment on 1st March, and I'll … be on the road a lot. You know. Meeting clients.'

'Dining out on someone else's credit card.' Ruth's voice cut in.

line 33 'There's more to it than that,' Claire responded quickly. Then, before Ruth could start the age-old argument, Claire consciously lowered her voice.

'Tell me the day you need me to have Sky, I'll check my diary.'

'Well, it's two days, actually.' Ruth sounded embarrassed.

Thinking about minding a six-year-old for two days almost made Claire choke. She gulped down her coffee and wondered if she could use the new assignment as an excuse.

There was something in Ruth's voice, though, that made her pause.

'Can't Mum take care of her? I thought Mum and Dad were the perfect grandparents?' It seemed odd to Claire that two people who had no time for their own children could go mad over someone else's, even if they were their grandkids.

'Er, Mum's coming with me, to the hospital.'

Ruth's words finally got through to Claire. 'Just what tests are you having exactly?'

'Weren't you listening? You never listen to me.'

Claire almost smiled at the petulant tone in Ruth's voice. For a moment they were twelve and fourteen again.

31 When Claire realises who is phoning her, she

    A expects to hear some good news.

    B tries to hide her true feelings.

    C hopes it will be a long conversation.

    D knows exactly what she will say to Ruth.

Tip! You don't need to understand every word of the text to be able to answer the questions, so don't spend too much time on expressions you don't know.

32 Why doesn't Claire know who is ill?

    A Ruth didn't make it clear who she was talking about.

    B None of her other relatives had written to her about it.

    C She was away on business when the illness began.

    D She wasn't paying attention when Ruth was speaking.

33 How does Claire feel about her school?

    A She would have achieved more at a better school.

    B Her parents never appreciated how successful she was there.

    C Her sister was better suited to that school than she was.

    D She may have been sent there for the wrong reasons.

Advice

31 Does a 'sigh' show that someone is happy or unhappy?

32 Look at the last sentences of both the second and third paragraphs.

33 Who does Claire seem to be criticising, apart from Ruth?

34 How does Claire react in the next paragraph, after 'Of course we can't afford that…'?

35 Look for the main subject of that part of the text.

36 Study Claire's thoughts between the dialogue with her sister.

34 What is Claire's attitude to Ruth's financial problems?

    A She feels they are largely Ruth's own fault.

    B She wishes she could do more to help Ruth.

    C She thinks Ruth could get any well-paid job she wanted.

    D She feels guilty about having more money than Ruth.

35 What does 'it' on line 33 refer to?

    A spending the firm's money

    B the task Claire has been given

    C looking after Ruth's daughter

    D the reason Claire sounds stressed

36 What do we learn about Claire and her family?

    A Her relationship with her sister has completely changed since their childhood.

    B She realises that her parents treated her very well when she was a child.

    C She doesn't understand why her parents are so close to their grandchildren.

    D She accepts that her mother is more interested in Ruth than in her.

Tip! Choose your answer according to what the text says, not what you think the correct answer should be from your general knowledge, or your own opinions.

Task information

- In Part 6 there is a text with six gaps (37–42). Each gap is for a missing sentence. These sentences are in a list (A–G), but in the wrong order. You have to put the sentences into the correct gaps.
- There is also a sentence that doesn't fit anywhere. This can be any of A–G.
- You can use each sentence A–G once only.

- Part 6 tests your understanding of the overall structure of the text, and the development of ideas, opinions and events.
- The instructions tell you what kind of text it is and what it is about.
- The text has a title, and often some background information below it.

Predicting text content; finding clues

1 Read the title and the sentence below it in *italics*. What do you think the text will be about?

2 Study the extract. Gap 37 has the correct answer (F) and the expressions which link sentence F to the text are underlined. Match each link in sentence F and an underlined part of the text, e.g. *biologists/the scientists*.

The flight of the bee

New research explains the mystery of why bees never seem to get lost.

Those who have studied bees have long wondered how they always manage to find their way home. No matter how strong the cross-winds, they never seem to get blown off course. Now, however, <u>biologists</u> believe they have discovered their secret – by using radar to <u>observe their flight patterns</u>.

| **37** | F |

To do <u>so</u>, they fitted bees with tiny electronic instruments, which enabled <u>the scientists</u> to <u>track all their movements over several kilometres</u>. What <u>this</u> showed <u>them</u> was that bees seem to know exactly how far the wind is blowing them off course, and they react to this by adjusting their flight direction accordingly.

Aircraft pilots do something similar, using computers to calculate wind speed and direction. | **38** | B | Bees, on the other hand, do the same thing by checking the position of the sun and watching how the ground appears to be moving below them. If the wind is affecting the way they are going, they change direction.

During this experiment, the researchers also discovered that the wind speed affects the height at which bees fly. On windy days, it appears, bees flying against the wind tend to fly lower than usual. | **39** | G | This, they found, is because it normally blows more strongly higher up. Bees flying in the same direction as the wind, however, can use this to save energy by flying at greater heights.

Advice

37 Look for words like 'one', 'do' and 'so' used to link ideas, e.g. There were six cakes. I ate one; They love surfing. I do, too; He says it's a good idea. I don't think so.

38 Underline vocabulary links, e.g. use of the same word in both main text and sentence, or words with similar or opposite meanings.

39 When you see a word like 'that' or 'it', decide what it refers to. Remember that it may refer backwards or forwards in the text.

3 Gaps 38 and 39 have also been completed with the correct sentence. Underline the expressions that link text and sentence.

Action plan

1 Read the instructions, the title and any background information. What kind of text is it? What's the topic?

2 Quickly read through the main text. What is each paragraph about?

3 Look quickly at sentences A–G. Do any of them obviously fit particular gaps?

4 For each gap 37–42, study the ideas and words that come before and after it.

5 Look for similar or contrasting ideas in the list of sentences.

6 In both the main text and sentences A–G, underline vocabulary links, reference words such as *this* or *her*, and linking expressions like *also, even though, one, do* and *so*.

7 When you have chosen your answers, read the complete text. Does it make sense?

1 Look quickly at the text on page 30.

   1 What kind of text is it and what is it about?

   2 What is each of the main paragraphs about?

2 Follow the exam instructions, using the advice to help you.

Tip! Before you choose a sentence, check that the verb forms, singular/plural, etc. in the main text all agree.

Tip! Each time you choose one of A–G, cross it out so that you don't have to keep reading through the whole list. This will save you time.

You are going to read an article about the new headquarters of the World Wide Fund for Nature (WWF). Six sentences have been removed from the article. Choose from the sentences **A–G** the one which fits each gap (**37–42**). There is one extra sentence which you do not need to use.

A Even so, it remains in an ugly corner of a fairly unattractive town centre.

B So even if you aren't particularly concerned about the environment, as energy costs rise you'll want to save money on fuel bills.

C Other such features include extensive glass to increase natural light, natural ventilation, rainwater in the toilets, and heat pumps that bring warm air up from 200 metres below.

D It is hoped their new home will be a living example of that.

E That means you can't put back forests that are gone, not for a century, and the population size is not going to shrink.

F If you want to do something, you have to persuade people of the world not to pollute.

G If humanity is to survive, they must have been thinking, it will do so living in buildings of this kind.

Advice

37 Look for a sentence containing references to the people and the place.

38 Find a reference to the positive idea expressed in the sentence before the gap.

39 Look for a sentence that adds more description of the building.

40 Which sentence begins with a contrast link that would fit here?

41 The sentence after the gap gives a reason for something stated in the missing sentence.

42 Which 'numbers' in the next sentence are likely to be 'increasing'?

The ultimate green home: the WWF's new headquarters.

Sandwiched between an incredibly ugly shopping centre and a busy main road, the environmentalist Sir David Attenborough, no less, is planting a tree and declaring: 'Today is a historic day.' He really means it.

Maybe our children's future will be an overheated, desert-like world, but if it's not, it will probably look a lot like this. The new, highly environmentally-friendly home of the World Wide Fund for Nature, a hemispherical glass tube standing above a council car park, was officially opened today, watched by a small but enthusiastic crowd. **37** [ ] .

Known as the 'Living Planet Centre', it has jumping panda animations that greet visitors to its WWF Experience, where schoolchildren can interact with Ocean, River, Forest and Wildlife Zones. Since the mid-20th century, many of the ideas behind humanity's attempts to protect animals and the natural world have been started by the WWF. **38** [ ] .

'The World Wide Fund for Nature is one of the great hopes for the world,' Sir David Attenborough said. 'This building enshrines that, and advertises it to the world.' The concrete is all recycled, as is the carpet and even most of the computer equipment, and there are many solar energy panels. **39** [ ] In addition, new habitats and plant species have been installed around the gardens, while indoors a home has been found for three tall trees.

The sense of total calm inside, from the high curved ceilings to the plants and trees, is all the more remarkable for the building's urban location. It has been built between a canal and a small area of woods listed as a Site of Special Scientific Interest. **40** [ ] The contrast gives us an idea of what might just be possible in the future.

The WWF was set up in 1961. The organisation originally fought to protect individual species, such as the Arabian oryx, from extinction. Eventually, the focus moved from individual species to ecosystems: all the living things in one area and the way they affect each other. Sir David, who is an ambassador for the WWF, said: 'Now, it's not just individual ecosystems. Now the change is to a global approach. **41** [ ] That is because the planet is one vast ecosystem. The WWF has been the leader in changing everyone's attitudes towards nature.'

Sir David is clear about the task ahead, and more importantly, unlike many environmentalists, he believes it is not too late to make a difference. 'You can't turn the clock back, of course. **42** [ ] But we can slow down the rate at which the numbers are increasing, we can cut down the carbon we put in the atmosphere,' he said. 'It's never happened before that the whole world has come together and made a decision. To go as far as we have done to reduce carbon is an impressive achievement. But you cannot have unlimited growth in a limited situation. You can't expand infinitely in a finite planet.

Task information

- In Part 7 there may be one long text divided into sections or a number of shorter texts.
- There are 10 questions which you match with the sections or short texts (**A**, **B**, **C**, etc.), according to the question at the top, e.g. *Which person* … .
- Part 7 tests your ability to find particular information in a text. You need to understand detail, attitudes and opinions in the questions, and find the part(s) of the text which express the same idea.

- The instructions tell you what kind of text it is and what it's about. It always has a title.
- The information you need may not be in the same order as the questions.
- There may be evidence for a particular answer in more than one sentence or part of a sentence.

Finding evidence; avoiding incorrect answers

1 Study questions 43–48 and extract C from a Part 3 text below. Match the underlined text with the correct question (44, 45 and 47) by drawing a line.

> **Tip!** There may be evidence for a particular answer in more than one sentence, or part of a sentence.

Which person

took up this means of transport for environmental reasons? **43** [ ]

feels that travelling this way is more comfortable than it was? **44** [C]

once arrived late at work because of transport delays? **45** [C]

dislikes having to travel surrounded by a lot of people? **46** [ ]

has to walk a considerable distance every day? **47** [C]

thinks they pay too much to travel to and from work? **48** [ ]

> **C** Shop assistant Laura Sánchez recently switched from the bus to the tram to get to work. 'I wasn't keen at first,' she says, 'because <u>the nearest stop is more than a kilometre from my house, and that's quite a long way on foot</u> twice a day. I also used to think that <u>trams were cold, noisy things with hard wooden seats, but when I saw how much nicer they are these days</u>, I decided to make the change. The only problem,' she adds, 'is that if one breaks down there's a complete tram jam. <u>One Monday morning I was stuck like that for over an hour, and my boss wasn't pleased.</u>'

2 Look at questions 43, 46 and 48. Which two are answered correctly by extract E below? Underline the parts of the text that tell you, and write the question numbers on the right. Which is not answered correctly by extract E? How do you know?

> **E** Justin Mackenzie works in the city centre and takes the train every day. 'It's handy for the office,' he says, 'but the fares keep going up and up and at this rate I'll have to think about using my car to come into town.' He thinks that would be 'crazy', pointing out that 'it was because of all the pollution it caused' that he gave up driving to work and started going by rail instead. 'I really wouldn't want to have to do that,' he says, adding: 'I don't even mind the fact that the rush-hour trains are so crowded, because at least it means there are fewer people using their cars.'

Action plan

1 Read the instructions and the title to find out what kind of text it is and the topic.
2 Quickly read the questions and underline the key words.
3 Go quickly through the first section to see which questions it answers.
4 When you find information that seems to answer a question, read the question again and study the evidence in the text carefully.

Tip! Different texts or parts of the text may contain similar ideas, but you have to read carefully to decide which say **exactly the same thing** as the questions.

Tip! You will need to use the same option for more than one question, e.g. four answers might all be A.

Follow the exam instructions, using the advice to help you.

You are going to read an article from a travel magazine. For questions **43–52**, choose from the sections (**A–D**). The sections may be chosen more than once.

Which section

recommends paying the entrance fee? **43** ☐

states that the beach has featured in advertisements? **44** ☐

says visitors may be surprised by the water temperature? **45** ☐

points out that the water is quite shallow? **46** ☐

suggests visitors should take photos of the beach? **47** ☐

says visitors can walk on the beach in their bare feet? **48** ☐

mentions a pleasant smell from the trees? **49** ☐

advises visitors to get to the beach early in the day? **50** ☐

states that it is not always possible to visit the beach? **51** ☐

warns visitors to the beach to protect their skin? **52** ☐

Advice

43 Look for a reference to money that must be paid.

44 Be careful: one paragraph only **imagines** it in an advertment.

45 Focus on the temperature of the water, not the air.

46 Look for a description of depth in relation to the human body.

47 Think of a short word for 'photos'.

48 Take care: on one beach this isn't a good idea.

49 Think of another word for 'smell'.

50 Make sure it is about the morning, not later on.

51 Look for a phrase that means in one season only.

52 What do sunbathers use to protect their skin?

Four of the world's best beaches

Which are the best beaches on Earth? Here are our top four.

A Rodas Beach, the Cies Islands, Spain

Some of Spain's most spectacular beaches lie in Galicia on the Atlantic coast, and perhaps the most stunning of these are on the Cies Islands. These unspoilt and uninhabited islands are a national park, with public access limited to the summer months, and contain the perfectly-shaped Rodas Beach with its pure white sand and clear blue sea. At first sight it almost seems tropical, until dipping your toe in the water encourages you to spend a lazy day on the beach rather than dive in for a swim. There you can enjoy the quiet, the warmth of the sun and the scent of pine from the nearby woods, and later on have an excellent meal in the reasonably-priced fish restaurant close to the beach.

B Whitehaven Beach, Whitsunday Islands, Australia

Australia is famous for wonderful beaches, and Whitehaven must surely be one of its very best. Set against a background of amazingly-green tropical forest, and with views across the clear blue ocean to distant small islands, the sandy white beach is like something from a picture postcard or a TV commercial. As you would expect in such a sunny climate, the water is pleasantly warm, ideal for swimming on or below the surface. The sand, in contrast, always remains cool as it is of a type that reflects the sunlight, so you won't need sandals. As the island has no permanent inhabitants, and most day trippers leave by boat quite early, in the late afternoon and evening you can have the place almost to yourself.

C Matira Beach, Bora Bora, Tahiti

Matira Beach on the Pacific island of Bora Bora has incredibly white sand, beautiful fish swimming in clear blue-green water, and stunning sunsets. The air temperature hardly varies around the year, and neither does that of the ocean – which is only waist-high even hundreds of metres from the shore. And unlike windier beaches nearby, Matira is quite well sheltered. There isn't, however, much shade, so it is advisable to use plenty of sun cream, and the sand can feel uncomfortably hot unless you wear beach shoes or something similar. There is no charge to visit the beach, yet it rarely becomes crowded at any time of day. Everyone should go there at least once in life, and when you do, make sure you have your photo taken as the sun goes down.

D Anse Source d'Argent Beach, Seychelles

This must be one of the most photographed beaches in the world, so don't forget to get some shots of your own, especially of the sea and the sand framed by the background of enormous pink rocks, with tall palm trees right behind them. It's easy to see why commercials have been made there. The patches of brilliantly white sand between those beautiful rocks make it the perfect place to spend a relaxing day, and it is well worth the small amount it costs for access. The best spots – those with both sunshine and shade – quickly get taken, so make sure you arrive well before the sun starts to beat down and the sand heats up.

 Tip! Don't expect to find answers in the text that use the same words as the questions. Look for words, phrases and sentences that express the same ideas.

Task information

- The essay task in Part 1 tests your ability to write an 'opinion' essay for the teacher of an English class.
- There is a question or statement to discuss and you are also given some notes to guide your writing. You should write between 140 and 190 words.
- You should allow about 40 minutes for this task, including time to plan your work and check for mistakes at the end.

- Your essay must be well organised into paragraphs, with good linking expressions.
- As your reader will be a teacher, you should use fairly formal language.
- You should write full sentences with correct grammar and punctuation, using a good range of language with accurate spelling.

Useful language: ordering points or reasons; adding information

1 Where would you use these linking expressions? Put them under the correct headings.

Finally,	First of all,	On balance,
In conclusion,	Next,	Lastly,
Last but not least,	To sum up,	Firstly,
Then	To begin with,	To conclude,
Secondly,		

for the first point	for further points	for the last point	in the conclusion
Firstly			

2 Some linking expressions are used at the beginning of a sentence, but some are not. Circle the correct words in italics.

1 In the city there are more places to go. *Also / Too*, they stay open later.
2 Working in a coal mine is a hard job. *Furthermore / As well*, it can be dangerous.
3 Travelling by train is more relaxing than driving. It is better for the environment, *besides / too*.
4 You have to find somewhere to play. *As well / As well as that*, you need to buy all the sports equipment.
5 In winter, the nights are much longer. *Too / In addition*, it is a lot colder then.
6 Making your own furniture is an enjoyable hobby. It saves money, *as well / in addition*.

Focusing on the question; text organization

1 Look at this exam task. Would you answer 'yes' or 'no' to the question?

In your English class you have been discussing animals. Now your teacher has now asked you to write an essay.

Write an essay, using **all** the notes and giving reasons for your point of view.

It is wrong to keep animals in zoos?
Notes Write about:
1 how the animals are treated 2 learning about the animals 3 .... (your own idea)

Write your answer in 140–190 words in an appropriate style.

2 Quickly read the essays on page 36 written by strong First candidates, A and B (language errors have been corrected). Ignore 1–10 and answer these questions about each essay.

  1 Does it include
* only arguments that answer 'yes' to the question, followed by the writer's opinion?
* only arguments that answer 'no' to the question, followed by the writer's opinion?
* arguments on both sides, followed by the writer's opinion?

  2 In which paragraph does the writer discuss note 1?

  3 Where does the writer discuss note 2?

  4 Which point is the writer's own idea?

3 Now read the essays again and complete questions 1–10 with the following notes. You can use the same note more than once.

* Writer's own opinion
* Gives an example
* Sums up points already made
* Expression that links points
* Gives a reason
* Tells the reader what to expect
* Contrast link

Essay A

In my opinion, keeping animals in zoos is not as cruel as people say – sometimes it is even useful – for three main reasons.

First of all, they take care of the animals, giving them the best food. The animals are cleaned every day and they live in good conditions. There is a large number of scientists that care for the animals, for instance if they catch a disease.

Secondly, there are some animals that are disappearing because they have been hunted without any control. At the zoo they are away from these hunters, so they are safe and it is possible to prevent them disappearing.

Finally, there is also an educational reason. Children can see different animals from all over the world alive and from my point of view this is the best way of learning. They also learn to take care of them and the most important thing, to love them.

In conclusion, I believe keeping animals in a zoo is no more cruel than keeping them at home. The only important thing is to care for them.

Writer's own opinion
Gives a reason
(1) Tells the reader what to expect
(2) ....
(3) ....
(4) ....
Sums up points already made

Essay B

Keeping animals in zoos is an important issue today because there are many people in favour of animal rights. In this essay I intend to examine the arguments for and against keeping animals in zoos.

One of the strongest arguments in favour is the fact that children can see animals from other countries. Consequently, visiting zoos can help them learn about nature. Furthermore, zoos can help protect some kinds of animals, which might be in danger of extinction.

On the other hand, there are several arguments against it. To begin with, it is known that animals in zoos suffer from loneliness since they are not living in their natural environment. Secondly, they do not behave as they would do if they were free, because they have to get used to a new way of living, even if they have been born in the zoo. Lastly, people can use them to carry out experiments.

On balance, I am not in favour of keeping animals in captivity because, as I have shown, that is like prison, which is very sad.

Outlines the background
Gives a reason
(5) ....
Says which side comes first
(6) ....
(7) ....
(8) ....
(9) ....
(10) ....

Action plan

1 Read the instructions, the question or statement, and the two notes you are given.

2 Decide whether to write for or against, or whether to give arguments both for *and* against.

3 Think of a third idea to add to the notes you are given. Write this down, then make a plan.

4 Write a short introductory paragraph, commenting generally on the topic, e.g. *The climate is changing, so many people are saying ...* . You can give your own opinion here and/or in your last paragraph.

5 Write in a fairly formal style, including linking expressions from *Useful language* on page 34.

6 Write at least two sentences about each main point, giving reasons and possibly also examples.

7 Give your opinion by summarising your main points in a concluding paragraph.

8 Check your essay for mistakes – and that you have written at least 140 words.

> **Tip!** Note down a few useful expressions for each paragraph, but don't write a full draft – you won't have time in the exam.

Read the exam task below.

1 Who are you writing for?

2 What must you write about?

3 What two main points must you include?

4 Which other main point will you add?

You have had a discussion in your English class about different ways of watching music concerts. Now your English teacher has asked you to write an essay.

Write an essay using all the notes and give reasons for your point of view.

Which is better: attending a concert, or watching the same concert at home, for example online or on TV?

Notes

Write about:

---

1 convenience

2 atmosphere

3 .... (your own idea)

> **Tip!** If you want to think of points you disagree with, imagine what someone who disagrees might say.

> **Tip!** If you are going to write for *and* against, list your points in two columns so you can balance the essay.

Write your answer in 140–190 words in an appropriate style.

In Part 2 (questions 2–4) you choose one writing task. The possible tasks are: email or letter, article, report and review. The email task is practised on page 42 in Test 1, the letter on page 87 in Test 2, the article on page 46 in Test 1 and page 93 in Test 2, the report on page 49 in Test 1, and the review on page 90 in Test 2.

Task information

- The email task often tests your ability to write to an English-speaking friend or colleague.
- You are asked to respond to a situation described in the question. In your email of 140–190 words you must include all the information asked for.
- You have about 40 minutes for this task, including time at the end to check your work.

- You have to organise your text into paragraphs, with a suitable beginning and ending.
- You must use an appropriate style and tone, depending on who your text is for.
- You need to write grammatically correct sentences with correct punctuation and spelling, and use a good range of language.

Useful language: formal and informal expressions

1 Decide whether A or B is more common in formal or informal writing.

   1 **A** full forms: *does not* .... *formal* ....
      B contracted forms: *doesn't* .... *informal* .....
   2 **A** phrasal verbs: *put off* ....
      B single-word verbs: *postpone* ....
   3 **A** use of exclamation marks: *I couldn't believe it!* ....
      B no exclamation marks: *I could not believe it.* ....
   4 **A** common words: *enough* ....
      B less common words: *sufficient* ....
   5 **A** long words: *frequently* ....
      B short words: *often* ....
   6 **A** active verb forms: *I took* ....
      B passive verb forms: *I was taken* ....
   7 **A** full forms of words: *approximately* ....
      B abbreviations: *approx.* ....
   8 **A** textbook expressions: *a limited quantity* ....
      B conversational expressions: *a bit* ....
   9 **A** friendly, personal tone: *Please try to …* ....
      B distant, impersonal tone: *It would be advisable to …* ....
  10 **A** complete sentences: *There was no sound.* ....
      B incomplete sentences: *Not a sound.* ....

2 Decide whether each of these expressions is formal or informal and whether it usually goes at the beginning or the end of a letter.

Example: **Don't forget to write soon.** *informal/end*

~~Don't forget to write soon.~~	Yours sincerely,	Hi Susana
Well, that's all for now.	Best wishes,	I apologise for the delay in replying.
It was great to get your email.	Dear Sir/Madam,	Give my love to everyone.
I have received your letter dated June 5.	Lots of love,	I look forward to hearing from you.
Thanks (very much) for your letter.	Dear Stefan,	Sorry to be so slow getting back to you.
This is just a quick note to say …		

3 Match the headings with groups of expressions 1–6. In each group there is one expression that is too formal for writing to a friend. Which is it?

Requesting information	Advising	Expressing enthusiasm
Changing the subject	~~Apologising~~	Expressing surprise

1 .... *Apologising* ....

Sorry about forgetting to tell you.
Please forgive me for making that mistake.
I would like to apologise for arriving so late.
It was silly of me to suggest that.

2 ....

Can you give me an idea when it'll finish?
I would be grateful if you could tell me the cost.
I'd like to know if you've got a spare ticket.
Could you let me know what time you'll be here?

3 ....

My advice to you is to consider it most carefully.
It'd be a good idea to try again.
I really think you should go somewhere else.
If I were you, I'd tell her now.

4 ....

That reminds me, it's her birthday next week.
By the way, what's his name?
With reference to the accommodation, there are certain changes …
Anyway, how's life in general?

5 ....

Believe it or not, I've just won the lottery!
Funnily enough, we were both at the same primary school.
I was most surprised to discover that the price has risen.
You'll never believe this, but she's his cousin!

6 ....

It's a really exciting place to go with friends!
I think it's great that everyone will be there!
I'm delighted to hear you won a prize!
I am extremely enthusiastic about learning Chinese.

4 Read this text written by a First candidate to a penfriend. It is well organised and there are no serious mistakes, but some of the expressions are too formal. Replace 1–8 with expressions from Exercise 2 and Exercise 3 on page 39.

Dear Emma,

(1) <u>I am writing to you in reply to your letter</u>. I'm very happy that you and your parents will stay in my country for a month.

(2) <u>I believe it is a good idea</u> that you will come to visit my city. I'm sure you will enjoy the holiday because (3) <u>it is an extremely</u> interesting place to visit.

(4) <u>In my opinion, I suggest that you</u> go and hear music in one of the main squares in the city centre. I'm sure you will enjoy it. Moreover, there are a lot of cultural places to visit and history museums too.

(5) <u>Next</u>, I believe it would be better to come in the first part of the month, because that is when there are fewer tourists and fewer people visiting the monuments and the museums.

(6) <u>To sum up</u>, (7) <u>I will be pleased to receive another letter from you soon</u>, Emma.

(8) <u>Yours sincerely</u>,

Carlos

Understanding instructions

1 Look at these exam instructions.

  1 Who has written to you?
  2 What is the situation?
  3 What questions does the writer ask you?

You have received this email from your English-speaking classmate Sam.

From: Sam

Subject: party plans

I'm pleased to say that all our classmates are able to come to the party we're organising for the end of the course. There are just a few more things I'd like to ask you. Should we hire a band for the occasion? Shall we order some food from a local restaurant? How about making it a fancy dress party?

Speak to you soon.

All the best,

Sam

Write your **email** in 140–180 words.

2 ⊙ **Read this text written by a strong First student and answer the questions.**

1 Is Anika's text well organized into paragraphs?
2 Does she answer all of Sam's questions? In which paragraphs?
3 Does she use the correct style and tone throughout?
4 How does she begin and end her email?
5 What reason for writing does she give?
6 How does she respond to the information Sam gives her?
7 How does she encourage Sam to write back?
8 Which linking expressions does she use for ordering points?
9 What kinds of informal language does she use?

Dear Sam,

I'm writing to answer your letter asking for my opinion on the end-of-course party preparations.

First of all, I'd like you to know how happy I am that everyone can come. We will be all together and I'm sure we'll have a wonderful time.

As far as food is concerned, I think it'd be better to ask everyone to bring some food so that we can save money. It would also be cheaper for us not to hire a band to play music at the party. We could sing on our own and have more fun.

In addition, your idea about a fancy dress party is fantastic! We could also indicate the theme of the party so that we could all be dressed up in the same kinds of costume.

I hope this has helped. I'm sure the party will be a great success.

Looking forward to hearing from you.

Very best wishes,

Anika

Action plan

1 Read the instructions and any text that is included in the question.

2 Who do you have to write to? Why? Which points must you include? Decide whether to use formal or informal language.

3 Think about the topic and your reader, and note down ideas. How many paragraphs will you need?

4 Make a plan and put your best ideas under short paragraph headings. Do they cover all the points in the question?

5 Note down some words or phrases for each paragraph, including expressions from the *Useful language* on pages 38–39, but don't try to write a complete draft.

6 Write your text. Keep to the topic and to your plan.

7 Use a wide range of vocabulary and grammar, and make sure your handwriting is easy to read.

8 Check your completed text. Have you made any careless mistakes? Is it at least 140 words? If not, you will lose marks.

1 **Look at the exam task below.**

1 Is Jamie's message written in a formal or an informal style?

2 What does he tell you about his sister and her friends?

3 What four things does he ask you?

You have received this email from your English-speaking friend Jamie.

From: Jamie

Subject: day trips

My sister and her friends are planning to spend next week in your area, and during their stay they would like to travel around a little.

Could you suggest somewhere interesting they could go for a day trip? What would be the best means of transport from your town? What time should they set off in the morning and when should they begin the return journey?

Thanks,

Jamie

Tip! Use your own words instead of expressions taken from the question, e.g. if it says *What's your opinion?*, write *my own feeling is …* or *I'd say …* .

Tip! If you make any mistakes, cross them out and write the corrections. It doesn't matter if you make a lot of corrections, as long as they are easy to read.

Tip! You may lose marks if you use the same expression all the time, e.g. instead of repeating *I want to*, say *I'd like to*, *what I'd enjoy is* or *it'd be good to …* .

Write your **email** in 140–190 words.

2 Follow the exam instructions and write your email. Remember to check your work for mistakes when you finish.

Task information

- The article task in Part 2 tests your ability to write an interesting text for a magazine or newsletter.
- You may need to write descriptions, give examples, make comments or give your opinions.
- You are writing for readers who are already interested in the topic.
- You should write **140–190** words.

Useful language: strong expressions

1   You can make your writing more interesting by using stronger expressions.
Replace the words in *italics* with the adjectives in the box.

awful	enormous	essential	exhausted	fantastic
fascinated	filthy	freezing	furious	terrified

1   By midnight, we were completely *tired*.
2   When I found out about it, I was *angry* with her.
3   The water was *cold*, so Holly swam quickly.
4   We all had a really *good* day at the theme park.
5   Matt was *afraid*, but he tried not to show it.
6   There are two *big* mountains on the island.
7   After playing rugby, Joe's shirt was *dirty*.
8   That nightclub is *bad* – the worst in town.
9   When you go diving, it is *important* to stay safe.
10 Visitors are *interested* by the ancient drawings.

2   Write a sentence of your own, using each of the words in the box in Exercise 1.

Focusing on instructions

1   Look at this exam task. What two things does the writer have to do?

You have seen this announcement on an English-language website.

My favourite sport

Tell us why you enjoy your favourite sport so much, and what people should do if they want to take it up.

We will publish the most interesting articles in the next few days.

Write your **article** in 140–190 words in an appropriate style.

2 Study these two articles written by First candidates (language errors have been corrected). For each question 1–12, write Yes or No under A, B or both A and B. Where possible, give a reason or example.

Which article

		A	B
1	has an interesting title and introduction?	No. Title too similar to task, dull introduction.	Yes. They catch readers' attention.
2	deals with both parts of the task?		
3	is well organised into paragraphs?		
4	is written in an informal style?		
5	makes good use of linking words?		
6	uses a good range of vocabulary?		
7	uses a good range of structures?		
8	gives relevant examples?		
9	includes the writer's opinions?		
10	describes personal experiences?		
11	asks the reader a question?		
12	has an interesting ending?		

3 Which article, A or B, got a better mark, do you think?

Article A

MY CHOICE OF SPORT

In this article I would like to explain why I decided, one day, to take up a certain sport. First of all, doing some sport is good for your health. This is obvious, but which kind of sport suits you? If you want to combine exercise with enjoyment, I can recommend volleyball.

One advantage is that you can play in a team, which can be really fantastic!

Also, volleyball is never boring, compared to endless hours in the gym.

For me, this game is an art where you have to use your skill and brain as well!

The main advice to anyone who would like to try this sport is to protect your joints! You can get high-quality equipment for this sport everywhere.

Secondly, you have to be cooperative with your teammates.

Last but not least, enjoy yourself!

Article B

DIVING DEEP

Are you too scared to try something new, something unusual which involves more risk than everyday sports? If not, go diving – you'll love it.

I am 21 and I've been scuba-diving for three years. It's not just a hobby for me; it's much more than that.

At first everybody is terrified of sinking into a deep, dark sea, because anything can happen, at any time. But you can't keep thinking about this, otherwise you'll miss a different, magical world down there.

Everybody says you can see all that on TV, but it's not the same. You have to see everything with your own eyes. It's wonderful when you discover something you have never seen before, such as a shark swimming. It is unbelievable.

I suggest everyone try scuba-diving at least once. It needs practice, maybe for three weeks, to be good at it, but a good instructor can help. You also have to buy your equipment. Ask somebody to help you if you don't know exactly what you need.

It's well worth it. I just know that everyone who decides to go scuba-diving will have a fantastic time!

Action plan

1 Read the instructions. Do you know enough about the topic to write an article?

2 Think about who your readers are and what they would like to read about.

3 Spend a few minutes making a plan based on all parts of the task, noting down points and language for each paragraph. Try to include adjectives from *Useful language* on page 43.

4 Think of a good title to attract your readers' attention, and an interesting introduction to make them want to keep reading.

5 Write your text in a lively way that will hold readers' interest. You can describe your own experiences and give your own opinions.

6 Use language that is fairly informal. Try to include some interesting expressions, e.g. *it's well worth it,* and perhaps questions like *I wonder what would happen if …*

7 Make the ending interesting by encouraging readers to think about what they have read.

8 Check your article for mistakes – and that you have written at least 140 words.

Study the exam question and write your answer in 140–190 words in an appropriate style.

You see this announcement in an English-language magazine.

22nd Century Fashion

What will clothes look like in 100 years' time?

Readers are invited to write articles saying what they think people will be wearing a century from now, and why.

The writer of the best article will receive a cash prize.

Tip! Prepare yourself for this task by reading articles in English in magazines or on the Internet.

Task information

- The report task tests your ability to give factual information and make recommendations or suggestions.
- The instructions include a description of a situation. You have to write a report of between 140–190 words.
- Allow about 40 minutes for this task, including time at the end to check your work.

- The report may be for a teacher or school director, or classmates, members of the same club, etc. You therefore have to write in an appropriate style.
- Organise your text into report format and use headings if needed.
- Write full sentences and try to use correct grammar and punctuation, with a good range of language with accurate spelling.

Useful language: report

Put these expressions under the correct headings. Can you think of more to add under each heading?

I would recommend that …	It would appear that …	In conclusion, …
This report looks at …	It is felt that …	The purpose of this report is to …
It is said to be …	It has been suggested that …	There would seem to be …
The aim of this report is to …	To sum up, …	I believe we should …
I (would) suggest …	I strongly recommend …	This report is intended to show that …

Introduction	Description and findings	Recommendations and suggestions	Conclusion

Understanding instructions

1   Study the exam instructions below and underline the key words.

  1 What is the situation?

  2 Who must you write a report for? Should the style be formal, informal or neutral (neither particularly formal nor informal)?

  3 What two things do the instructions say you *must* do?

  4 What else *should* you write, do you think?

> You have had a class discussion about sports and your teacher has asked you to suggest a sport that could be played at your college. Describe a sport that you have tried and say why you think it would be popular with students.
>
> Write your **report** in 140–190 words in an appropriate style.

2 The answer below was written by Tomasz, a First Certificate candidate.
Quickly read his report and think of a title for it.

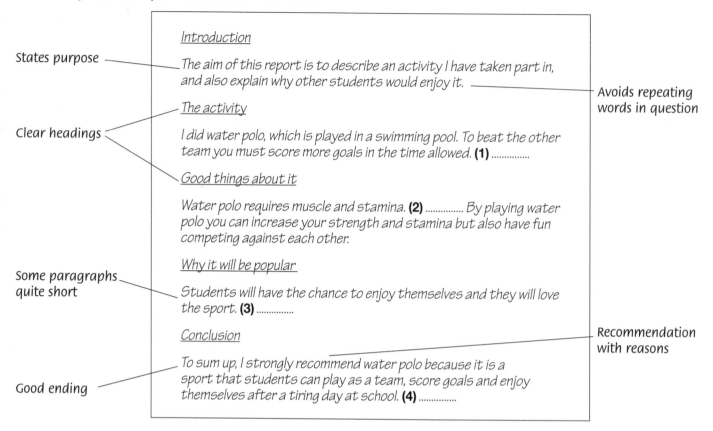

States purpose

Clear headings

Some paragraphs
quite short

Good ending

Introduction

The aim of this report is to describe an activity I have taken part in, and also explain why other students would enjoy it.

The activity

I did water polo, which is played in a swimming pool. To beat the other team you must score more goals in the time allowed. **(1)** ....

Good things about it

Water polo requires muscle and stamina. **(2)** .... By playing water polo you can increase your strength and stamina but also have fun competing against each other.

Why it will be popular

Students will have the chance to enjoy themselves and they will love the sport. **(3)** ....

Conclusion

To sum up, I strongly recommend water polo because it is a sport that students can play as a team, score goals and enjoy themselves after a tiring day at school. **(4)** ....

Avoids repeating
words in question

Recommendation
with reasons

3 Study the notes next to Tomasz's report. Then add sentences A–D in the correct gaps 1–4.

A I therefore suggest it should become a college sport.

B In addition, it would appear that there are no local water polo clubs.

C Although this is only 30 minutes, for the players it seems much longer.

D In fact, it is said to be the most physically demanding of all sports.

4 Read the completed report.

1 Is it either too short or too long for Writing Part 2?

2 Is it well organised? How many paragraphs does it have?

3 Does it answer both parts of the question? In which paragraphs?

4 Is it written in an appropriate style?

5 Are there any language errors?

6 Which expressions from *Useful language* on page 47 does the writer use?

7 Do you think this report would get full marks?

Action plan

1 Read the instructions. Do you know enough facts about the topic to write a report on it?

2 Decide who will read your report and what they will want to know.

3 Think about any knowledge and/or personal experience you could mention, and note down some ideas.

4 Decide if you will use headings, and think of a good title that indicates the content of the report.

5 Spend a few minutes making a plan based on all parts of the task, including recommendations or suggestions.

6 Write your text in a style that is appropriate for your readers. Try to make it interesting; if possible, include some facts that may be new to them.

7 Try to use expressions from *Useful language* on page 47 in each part of your report.

1 Read the exam task below.

> **Tip!** In your first paragraph, say what the purpose of the report is.

1 Who is your report for?

2 What *two* things do you have to do?

You see this announcement on a college notice board.

Reports wanted

This College is always keen to make improvements to the facilities available to students, staff and visitors. The Director therefore invites you to write a report describing the current condition of <u>one</u> of the following, and suggesting ways it could be improved:

- the reception area
- the library
- the cafeteria.

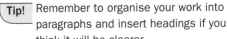

---

2 Write your **report** in 140–190 words in an appropriate style.

> **Tip!** Remember to organise your work into paragraphs and insert headings if you think it will be clearer.

Task information

- In Part 1 you hear eight short unrelated extracts from monologues or exchanges. There is one multiple-choice question per extract, each with three options. You hear each extract twice.

- Part 1 tests your understanding of: gist, detail, opinion, attitude, function, purpose, relationship, topic, place, situation, agreement, etc.

- The question includes information about the situation (e.g. a phone call, a radio programme, an extract from a play, etc.) followed by a direct question (e.g. *How does she feel?*).

Understanding distraction

1 Study this multiple-choice question and the recording script below. Why is B correct? Why are A and C wrong?

You hear a man talking about buying a bicycle.
What most attracted him to this bike?

A its special features

B its condition

C its price

'I saw it advertised in the local newspaper and I thought I'd ring the seller to see if it was still for sale and <u>whether he'd drop the price because it seemed a bit high to me.</u> He wouldn't, but I liked the sound of it and we arranged a time for me to call round later. Well as soon as I saw it, I knew I had to have it. <u>It was just an ordinary bike really, nothing remarkable about it at all</u>, but <u>it'd obviously been very well looked after. It was a few years old, but you really couldn't tell.</u> So I bought it there and then.'

C — (line pointing to price sentence)
A — (line pointing to ordinary bike sentence)
B — (line pointing to well looked after sentence)

> **Tip!** Don't choose your answer until you've heard the whole text at least once.

2a 🎧 02 Look at the next question and listen twice to the recording. Which is the correct answer, A, B or C? Why?

You overhear a conversation in a café between two people.
Why didn't she call him?

A She didn't have his number.

B It was too late in the evening.

C Her phone wasn't working.

b 🎧 02 Listen again. Why are the other two answers wrong?

> **Tip!** You won't hear the same words as the words in the question, so listen for the same idea.

Action plan

1 For each question, quickly read the first line. What's the situation? Will you hear one person or two? Female or male?

2 Look at the direct question and stem (e.g. *Who is the woman?*) and underline the key words.

3 When you first hear the recording, try to think of an answer to each question in your own words. Then choose (from **A**, **B** or **C**) the option most like your answer.

4 Check your answer the second time you listen, making sure that you have not made a mistake – speakers may use words connected with more than one option.

5 If you're still not sure which is the correct answer, cross out any you are sure are wrong and guess.

6 When the recording has finished and you have chosen your answer, forget about that question and concentrate on the next one.

 03 **Follow the exam instructions, using the advice to help you.**

You will hear people talking in eight different situations. For questions **1–8**, choose the best answer (**A**, **B** or **C**).

Tip! Before you listen, think of other expressions for the words in the question, e.g. 'What does he do?' – *he works in …, his job is …, he's employed as …,* etc.

Tip! Make sure you always know which question and situation you are listening to.

---

1 You hear a customer talking to a shop assistant about a coat she bought.

What does she want?

A a different kind of item

B the same item but in a different size

C her money back

2 You hear a weather forecast on the radio.

Tomorrow, the weather in the east of the country will be

A stormy in the morning.

B sunny in the afternoon.

C foggy in the evening.

3 You hear an office worker talking about cycling to work.

What does she enjoy most about it?

A getting some exercise each morning

B avoiding the traffic into town

C thinking about the day ahead

4 You hear a radio announcer talking about a competition for writers of short stories.

The man says that one of the rules is that

A you have to be over sixteen to enter.

B you can submit more than one entry.

C your entry must be emailed.

Advice

1 Be careful with the assistant's suggestions. The customer rejects two of these.

2 You need to listen for the correct region, weather and time of day.

3 Listen for an activity similar to one of those in A–C.

4 Don't be misled by numbers that seem to give the answer.

5 You hear a conversation about reading.

The man enjoys reading books which

A have characters that remind him of people he knows.

B describe situations that he finds highly amusing.

C are set in places that he is unlikely ever to visit.

6 You hear two people talking about watching films on the Internet.

What do they agree about?

A the advantages of buying films online

B the usefulness of reading film reviews

C the pleasure of watching films at home

7 You hear a woman at an airport talking on the phone.

Why did she miss her flight?

A She was held up by traffic.

B There was a long queue at check-in.

C She went to the wrong terminal.

8 You hear a man talking about his new job.

What attracted him to this job?

A the type of work

B the opportunities for promotion

C the salary offered

Advice

5 Remember that the question is about the present.

6 Both mention all of A–C, but the woman disagrees about two of them.

7 Base your answer on what happened this time, not on a previous occasion.

8 Listen to everything the speaker says about each point.

Task information

- In Part 2 you will hear a monologue lasting three to four minutes.
- Part 2 tests your understanding of detail, stated opinion and specific information.
- You have to listen for particular words, phrases or numbers to complete ten sentences. You should write these down exactly as you hear them.
- The 1–3 words you have to write will not be above First level.
- Sometimes words or names may be spelt out. If so, you must spell them correctly.
- All the questions follow the order of the information in the recording, and for each one you will hear a 'cue' that indicates an answer is coming.

Thinking about possible answers; listening for cues

Tip! Be careful with words, phrases or numbers you hear which may seem to fit the gaps, but are not correct.

1 Study exam question 9 and the extract from the recording script below. Why is *a child* correct in question 9? Would any other answer be possible? What mistakes might a candidate listening to this make? Why?

Rabbits are not suitable pets for ......*a child*...... **(9)** as they need a lot of care.

Tip! You may need to write three words, but often you need only write one or two.

Rabbits are clean, intelligent and friendly animals, and they make excellent pets. They do, though, require a considerable amount of attention in order to keep them healthy, comfortable and safe, so (9) it is better if an adult or a teenager, rather than a child, looks after them. As they are such sociable animals, preferring to live in pairs or groups, it is advisable to have at least two.

cue (similar to need a lot of care)

correct answer

2a 🎧 04 Look at question 10 below and listen twice to the extract from the same recording.

Inside the house, you should remove any .... **(10)** to keep the rabbits safe.

b Write the correct answer.

c 🎧 04 Listen again. What is the cue? Which other phrase could be mistaken for the correct answer?

Action plan

1 Read the instructions to get an idea of the situation.
2 Quickly go through the incomplete sentences, including the words after the gaps. This will help you get an idea of what the text is about.
3 For each gap, decide what kind of information (e.g. *object*, *number*) you need to listen for.
4 The first time you listen, write your answer in pencil, in case you want to change it on the second listening.
5 When the recording has finished, check the sentences all make sense – and check your spelling, too.

🎧 05 **Follow the exam instructions, using the advice to help you.**

You will hear an expert snowboarder called Brad Mitchell talking about the sport of extreme snowboarding. For questions **9–18**, complete the sentences with a word or short phrase. **[You will need to play this recording twice.]**

Extreme snowboarding

Brad says there are no **(9)** .... to warn extreme snowboarders of dangers.

Brad advises snowboarders always to follow the **(10)** .... when descending.

Brad always wears a **(11)** .... when he goes into the mountains.

According to Brad, you need a lot of **(12)** .... to set off down the mountain.

Brad particularly enjoys doing several **(13)** .... when he is going down a slope.

Brad says at first he found it difficult to do a good **(14)** .... on steep slopes.

Brad says you must never **(15)** .... if you feel you're about to fall.

Brad advises against putting your weight on your **(16)** .... in a fall.

Brad always carries a **(17)** .... in case he is in difficulty following a fall.

In the future, Brad would most like to try **(18)** .... snowboarding.

Advice

9 Listen for an expression that means 'there are no'.

10 Listen for expressions often used for giving advice.

11 Focus on what Brad does, not other people.

12 Don't be misled by what others say. Wait for Brad's opinion.

13 Make sure you choose the word that goes with the verb 'do'.

14 Which is the more difficult of the two skills mentioned?

15 Listen for an expression with a similar meaning to 'if you feel you're about to fall'.

16 Take care when the speaker mentions different parts of the body.

17 Focus on what Brad carries, not on what may be recommended.

18 Don't be misled by two other activities he mentions.

Task information

- In Part 3 you hear five short related monologues.
- Part 3 tests your understanding of: gist, detail, opinion, attitude, function, purpose, relationship, topic, place, situation, agreement, etc.
- The instructions you see and hear include information about the link between the five recordings.
- The eight options (A–H) do not usually follow the order of the information in the recording.

Dealing with distraction

1 Study this exam task and the recording script for Speaker 1 below. Why is C correct for question 19? Why are A and G wrong?

You will hear five different people talking about unfortunate events. For questions **19–23**, choose from the list (**A–H**) what each speaker says. Use the letters only once. There are three extra letters which you do not need to use.

A having something stolen

B falling over

C arriving late for work

D being hurt in an accident   Speaker 1 ☐ C ☐ 19

E failing a test   Speaker 2 ☐ ☐ 20

F breaking something valuable

G missing a train

H losing a ticket

> I kept looking at my watch and I realised I wasn't going to make it. They'd told me that if I didn't get in on time this morning, I'd have to look for another job, so —— C
> this was a disaster. But it was so unfair. I'd done everything right: I'd got up at
> 7.30, left the house at 8 and caught the early train into town. It was just my bad —— G
> luck that it broke down as soon as it left the station. I thought of calling to explain
> what'd happened, but I couldn't find my phone and at first I thought a thief must —— A
> have taken it. Then I remembered that in my hurry to go out, I'd left it on the
> kitchen table.

2a 🎧 06 Listen twice to Speaker 2 and answer question 20. Which is the correct answer, A, B, D, E, F or G? Which parts of the text tell you?

Tip! Before you answer a question, wait until you have heard everything the speaker has to say.

b 🎧 06 Listen again. Which two sentences might *seem* to be correct, but are not? Why are they wrong?

Tip! Listen for ideas, not just individual words, that are similar to those in A–H.

Action plan

1 Quickly read the instructions and options A–H. What is the link between the five recordings?

2 Study options A–H and underline the key words in each.

3 Before you listen, think of words or phrases that the speakers might use to talk about different aspects of the topic.

4 The first time you hear the recording, listen for the general idea of what each speaker says.

5 Choose the answer to each question that you think is correct.

6 The second time you listen, check that each of your choices exactly matches what the speaker says.

1 07 **Follow the exam instructions, using the advice to help you.**

You will hear five short extracts in which people talk about habits they find difficult to control.

For questions **19–23**, choose from the list (**A–H**) the habit each person has. Use the letters only once. There are three extra letters which you do not need to use. **[You will need to play this recording twice.]**

Tip! Be careful if a speaker says something connected with two or more options: there is only one correct answer.

A   eating unhealthy food

B   doing too much exercise

C   buying unnecessary items

D   watching too much television

E   spending too much time online

F   oversleeping

G   working too hard

H   arriving late for everything

Speaker 1 [   ] **19**

Speaker 2 [   ] **20**

Speaker 3 [   ] **21**

Speaker 4 [   ] **22**

Speaker 5 [   ] **23**

Tip! When you have chosen an answer, cross it out in pencil so that you can concentrate on the others.

Advice

A Be careful – one person buys unhealthy food but doesn't eat it.

B Four speakers mention exercise or sport, but only one says they do too much.

C Three speakers talk about shopping, but only one buys unnecessary items.

D Watching TV is mentioned by three speakers, but only one watches too much.

E One speaker mentions spending a lot of time online, but is referring to other people.

F Four speakers talk about their sleeping habits, but do any of them sleep too much?

G Take care with different meanings of 'work' and 'job'.

H Listen for someone who's late for everything, not just one thing.

Task information

- In Part 4 you will hear an interview or an exchange between two speakers lasting three to four minutes. There are seven multiple-choice questions, each with three options.
- Part 4 tests your understanding of: attitude, opinion, gist, main ideas and specific information.
- All the questions follow the order of the information in the recording; each part of the recording relates to a particular question.
- The instructions you see and hear may include information such as the main speaker's name, occupation or hobby, and/or the setting (e.g. a radio interview). This can tell you the type of language and information you might hear.

Understanding distraction; listening for cues

1 Study this multiple-choice question and the extract from the recording script. It is from a radio interview in which Dave Harris asks Lucy Williams about her work as a police officer. Why is A correct? Why are B and C wrong?

1 How does Lucy feel about her work now?

  A She likes the fact that she never gets bored.

  B She dislikes having to deal with aggressive people.

  C She would prefer to work in an office.

Dave	So tell me, Lucy, <u>what have you found to be the positive things about police work? What's the negative side to it?</u> `Cue`
Lucy	Well, I often come into contact with people who are upset or angry, maybe causing trouble, and I have to calm them down and in some cases make it clear I'm in authority. But <u>I just see that as part of the job, and in fact I'd probably miss it</u> if I were given <u>a desk job. I'd find that really dull</u> compared to being out on the street, which is <u>always interesting because no two days are ever the same. You never know what to expect next, and that's great</u>.

(Annotations in margin of extract: **B**, **C** beside "I just see that as part of the job..." / "a desk job. I'd find that really dull"; **A** beside "always interesting because no two days are ever the same.")

2a 🎧 08 Look at the next question and listen twice to the extract from the same interview. Which is the correct answer, A, B or C? Why?

2 What advice does she give to teenagers?

  A join the police instead of going to university

  B begin by working part-time for the police

  C do a different job before joining the police

b 🎧 08 Listen again. What is the cue? Why are the other two answers wrong?

> **Tip!** For every question you will hear a 'cue' – words that express a similar idea to the question – that tells you the answer is in that part of the recording.

> **Tip!** The options use phrases or sentences that rephrase, summarise or report the ideas in the text.

Action plan

1 Quickly read the instructions. What kind of recording is it? What's the topic? Who will you hear?

2 Before you listen, look at the first line of each item. What kind of information, e.g. somebody's opinion, do you need for each?

3 Underline the key words in each item to help you focus on the information you need.

4 Listen for expressions with similar or opposite meanings to the key words you underlined.

5 Think of an answer in your own words. Then choose the option most like your answer.

6 Check all your answers on the second listening.

🎧 09 **Follow the exam instructions, using the advice to help you.**

Tip! After you hear the instructions, there's a one-minute pause before the recording begins. Use this time to look through the questions, underlining the key words.

You will hear Leonie Steiner talking to an interviewer about her work as a music teacher in a school. For questions **24–30**, choose the best answer (**A, B** or **C**). **[You will need to play this recording twice.]**

24 Leonie first starting learning the piano
   A with a relative.
   B at primary school.
   C with a private teacher.

25 Leonie started giving music lessons
   A for the pleasure of seeing others learn.
   B because she needed some extra money.
   C to see if she was suited to teaching.

26 Leonie most likes to teach students who
   A have great natural talent at an early age.
   B need good teaching to develop their talent.
   C have previously been taught badly.

27 Leonie thinks that schools should
   A employ far more music teachers.
   B buy good musical instruments.
   C ensure that all their pupils pass music exams.

28 Leonie thinks the problem with singing in schools is that
   A many students are too embarrassed to sing.
   B few students want to learn how to sing.
   C singing is not often taught in them nowadays.

29 Leonie believes her success as a music teacher is a result of
   A choosing a particular age group of children to teach.
   B the training she received as a student teacher.
   C a natural ability to communicate with young people.

30 What decision did Leonie find difficult to make?
   A to turn down the offer of a job abroad
   B to refuse promotion in the school
   C to continue teaching when she felt tired

Advice

24 Listen carefully to the order in which she did things.

25 Don't be misled by reasons other people have for teaching.

26 Listen for a comparative form which tells you which she likes most.

27 Take care with ideas she mentions but then rejects. Which of A–C does she reject?

28 Think of another way of saying 'too embarrassed'.

29 What does the use of the past conditional tell you about something in the past?

30 Focusing on the word 'that' can help you decide about two of A–C.

Task information

- Part 1 lasts about two minutes.
- One of the examiners tells you their names and asks for yours. Then you give him/her your mark sheet.
- You answer questions from one of the examiners.
- You don't usually talk to the other candidate.
- Part 1 tests your ability to give basic information about yourself and to talk about everyday topics such as your work or studies, your family, your free time and your future plans.

- One aim of Part 1 is to help you relax by getting you to talk about a topic you know a lot about: yourself.
- To find out how your speaking will be assessed, go to the Cambridge English Language Assessment website.

Useful language: basic expressions

1 Write the expressions in the box next to the correct purpose.

also	and often	as well as that	because
~~for example~~	for instance	like	Pardon?
so	such as	the reason is	
Could you say that again, please?			
Sorry, I didn't catch that.			

To give an example: ....for example..........
To give a reason: ....
To add information: ....
To ask for repetition: ....

2 🎧 10 You will hear two candidates, Hanif and Yara, doing Part 1. Read the examiner's questions, then listen and decide which of statements 1–6 are true. Write Yes or No for each person.

Examiner's questions
Where are you from?
What do you like about living in your home town?
What sort of things do you do in your free time?
In what ways do you think you will use English?

		Hanif	Yara
1	sounds quite confident	No	....
2	is generally easy to understand	....	....
3	gives full answers to the questions	....	....
4	uses quite a wide range of language	....	....
5	is polite to the examiner	....	....
6	probably gets a good mark for Part 1	....	....

3 🎧 10 Listen again. Which of the expressions from Exercise 1 do they use?

Action plan

1 Be polite and friendly when you meet the examiners and the other candidate.

2 Listen carefully to the examiner's questions. If you don't understand something, politely ask him or her to repeat it (e.g. *Could you repeat that, please?*).

3 Don't just reply *yes* or *no* to the questions.

4 Don't try to give a speech or repeat sentences that you prepared earlier.

5 Make sure you speak loudly and clearly enough for the examiners and your partner to hear you. Be confident!

6 When you can, give reasons and examples in your answers.

7 Try to use a wide range of grammar and vocabulary.

If you have a partner, answer these questions in pairs.

Tip! While you are speaking, look at the examiner who asks you the questions, not at the other candidate.

Part 1	2 minutes (3 minutes for groups of three)
Interlocutor	First, we'd like to know something about you.

- Where are you from?

- What do you most like about the house or apartment where you live?

- Which do you think is the best day of the week? Why?

- What do you usually do on your birthday?

- How often do you watch TV?

- Tell us about a TV programme you really like.

Task information

- In Part 2 each candidate is given a one-minute 'long turn'. Nobody will interrupt you.
- The examiner gives each of you two pictures and will ask you to compare them, and answer a question which is written at the top of the page.

- This part tests your ability to organise your speaking, and to compare, describe and give your opinions.
- You also talk for 30 seconds about your partner's pictures, after their minute has finished.

Useful language: comparing and contrasting

1   Study pictures A and B on page C1, then write these headings above the correct groups of sentences (1–5).

> Guessing   Contrasting the pictures   Saying which you'd prefer to do
> Comparing the pictures   Saying which picture you're talking about

1 ....

The picture at the top shows people doing an exercise class.
In the second photo, there are some people playing tennis.
In the one at the bottom, there's a match going on.
They both show people taking part in sports.
In both of them there are people doing sports.

2 ....

He **seems/looks** a bit worried at the moment.
He **looks as if** he's going to win the match.
They **look like** professional tennis players
They **might/may/could be** playing in an important final.
Perhaps/Maybe it's been a very long match.
It's **probably** going to finish soon.

3 ....

I think the tennis players **are** fitt**er than** the people in the exercise class.
Playing tennis like that is **more** excit**ing than** doing an exercise class.
These people are moving much **more** quick**ly than** those people.

4 ....

Tennis is a competitive sport, **but** an exercise class isn't.
An exercise class is usually an indoor activity, **while** tennis is usually played outside.
Those people are playing to win, **whereas** the others are doing it to get fit.
They get paid for taking part. **On the other hand**, these people have to pay to do this.
You need a proper court to play tennis. **In contrast**, you can do this kind of exercise anywhere.

5 ....

I prefer to do exercise with lots of other people.
I enjoy fast-moving sports **more than** slower activities.
I'd rather do something non-competitive.
I find racket sports **more** fun **than** doing the same exercise again and again.

2 You will hear two candidates, Sofia and Riccardo, talking about two pictures in Speaking Part 2. Read these instructions and the question above photos A and B on page C2. What *two* things does Sofia (Candidate A) have to do? What does Riccardo (Candidate B) have to do?

Part 2   4 minutes (6 minutes for groups of three)

(Candidate A), it's your turn first. Here are your photographs on page C2. They show **young people with others who are close to them.**

I'd like you to compare the photographs, and say **why the two different kinds of relationship are important to teenagers.**

(Candidate B), **do you prefer to spend your free time with family or with friends?**

3a Look at the photos and think about the instructions. Which of these things do you think Sofia should and shouldn't do? Put a ✓ or a ✗ next to 1–10. Give reasons for the things she *shouldn't* do.

1 Say what each person in both pictures is wearing.
2 Suggest who the different groups of people might be.
3 Say what the two groups are doing at the moment.
4 Contrast the ages of the people in the two pictures.
5 Talk about what the people might do next.
6 Give examples of the things young people can do with friends.
7 Give reasons why young people need to have friends.
8 Describe her own family and her closest friends.
9 Give examples of the things young people can do with their family.
10 Say why young people sometimes need their family's support.

b 🎧 11 Now listen to the recording and check whether Sofia only talked about the things you ticked.

4 🎧 11 Listen again. Tick ✓ the expressions similar to those in *Useful language* on page 61 that Sofia and Riccardo use. Which expressions do they use to introduce reasons and examples?

Action plan

1 Listen to the instructions, study the pictures and read the question.

2 Think about what you're going to say. Imagine you're briefly describing the pictures to somebody who can't see them.

3 Don't speak *too* quickly, or for less than a minute. The examiner will say when it's time to stop.

4 Don't try to describe every detail. Just say what's similar and different about the pictures.

5 If you can't name something in the pictures, use other words (e.g. *the thing you use for …*).

6 When you answer the examiner's question, give your opinion, with reasons and examples.

7 Never interrupt your partner in Part 2. Listen carefully, so you can comment afterwards when the examiner asks you a question.

---

1 Look at the exam instructions below and photos A and B on page C3.
   1   What two things do you (Candidate A) have to do?
   2   What does your partner (Candidate B) have to do?
   3   What will you say about the pictures?
   4   How will you answer the question above the pictures?

2 If you have a partner, do this exam task in pairs. Remember that A talks for one minute, B for 30 seconds.

> In this part of the test, I'm going to give each of you two photographs. I'd like you to talk about your photographs on your own for about a minute, and also to answer a question about your partner's photographs.
>
> *Candidate A)*, it's your turn first. Here are your photographs on page C3. They show **different places where fruit and vegetables are sold.**
>
> I'd like you to compare the photographs, and say **why you think people choose to shop in these different places.**
>
> *(Candidate B)*, **Which of these places would you rather buy fruit and vegetables in?**

Tip! If you make a mistake, it's fine to correct yourself, but then continue talking and complete the task.

Tip! Make sure you spend enough time on both comparing the photos and answering the question about them.

3 Look at the exam instructions below and photos A and B on page C4.
   1   What two things does your partner (Candidate B) have to do?
   2   What do you (Candidate A) have to do?
   3   What could your partner say to compare and contrast the pictures?
   4   How do you think he or she will answer the question above the pictures?
   5   How will you answer the question the examiner asks you (Candidate A)?

Tip! Before the exam, get lots of practice talking about pictures. A minute can seem like a long time!

4 If you have a partner, do this exam task in pairs.

> Now, *(Candidate B)*, here are your photographs on page C4. They show **people who are related to each other.**
>
> I'd like you to compare the photographs, and say **how important you think the relationship is to the different people.**
>
> *(Candidate A)*, **Do you spend more of your free time with family or with friends?**

Task information

- Part 3 lasts four minutes. You work in pairs.
- The examiner gives you a piece of paper with written prompts that show different ideas or possibilities, and tells you what you have to do.
- First you talk about the prompts together, giving your opinions. Then the examiner asks you to try to make a decision.

- This part tests your ability to talk about different possibilities, make suggestions, express opinions and give reasons, agree or disagree, and attempt to decide together.
- You take turns so that your partner and you spend about the same amount of time speaking.

Useful language: suggestions

Complete the headings above each group of expressions (1–5) with these words.

> Agreeing with   Asking if someone agrees with
> Disagreeing politely with
> Giving reasons for disagreeing with   Making

1 .... **suggestions**
How about ...?
Why don't we ...?
Perhaps we should ...?
What do you think ...?
So shall we ..., then?

2 .... **suggestions**
Don't you think so?
Would you agree?
Wouldn't you say so?
Is that all right with you?
Would you go along with that?

3 ....**suggestions**
Right.
I think so, too.
That's true.
I completely agree with you.
That's a great idea.

4 .... **suggestions**
I'm not really sure about that.
I think it might be better to ...
I think I'd rather ...
I don't really agree. I think ...
I'm not so keen on ...

5 .... **suggestions**
That's because ...
For one thing, ... (for another ...)
Well, the thing is ...
I think the problem is that ...
The main reason is that ...

Focusing on instructions and pictures; listening for expressions

1 Look at the exam instructions below and the diagram.

  1 What is the topic of the discussion?

  2 What two things do you have to do?

Here are some things that you often find in the home and a question for you to discuss.

Now, talk to each other about how useful these things are to people.

Now you have a minute to decide which two things are most important to you.

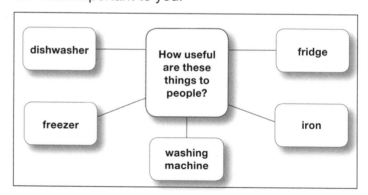

2 🎧 1 12 Listen to two candidates, Eleni and Stanislaw, doing this task and answer questions 1–7 with *Yes* or *No*.

  1 Do they listen and reply to each other? ....Yes...

  2 Do they disagree politely? ....

  3 Do they give reasons and examples? ....

  4 Do they discuss each object? ....

  5 Do they take turns talking? ....

  6 Do they try to decide on two objects? ....

  7 Do they agree? ....

3 🎧 1 12 Listen again and tick ✓ the expressions similar to the *Useful language* on the left.

Action plan

1 Listen carefully to the instructions and look at the diagram with your partner.

2 Start the discussion with something like *Would you like to start, or shall I?* or *Shall we begin with this one?*

3 Begin by talking about one of the things, giving your opinion, or perhaps making a suggestion. Then ask what your partner thinks, and why.

4 Talk briefly about each thing. Reply to your partner's ideas and give reasons for your suggestions, opinions and preferences. If you disagree with him or her, be polite.

5 Listen again to the examiner and then begin the decision-making by saying, for example, *So which do you think would be best?* or *Which shall we go for?*

6 Try to decide which to choose (e.g. *Shall we do this one?* or *I'm in favour of that one*).

7 If you agree, say something like *Right, that's what we'll do.* If you can't decide, you can say *Shall we leave it at that, then?* or simply *Let's agree to disagree.*

---

1 Study the exam instructions below and the diagram on page C5.

  1 What do you have to imagine?

  2 What two things do you have to do?

  3 How many suggestions are there and what is each called?

Tip! Don't try to reach a decision too quickly – you have a full minute to do this.

2 If you have a partner, do this exam task in pairs.

Tip! Keep the conversation going, for instance by saying *What do you think of this idea?* or *Let's talk about the next one.*

> **Part 3**
>
> **Interlocutor** Now, I'd like you to talk about something together for about two minutes.
> *(3 minutes for groups of three)*
>
> I'd like you to imagine that a restaurant is trying to attract more customers. Here are some of the ideas they are considering and a question for you to discuss.
>
> First you have some time to look at the task.
>
> Now, talk to each other about why these ideas might attract more customers to the restaurant.
>
> Thank you. Now you have a minute to decide which idea might attract the most customers.
>
> Thank you.

Tip! Don't speak for a long time without letting your partner speak. You may lose marks if you don't take turns.

Task information

- Part 4 lasts four minutes. You answer questions based on the same topic as Part 3.
- This part tests your ability to talk about issues in more depth than in the other three parts of the Speaking paper. You will need to express opinions and give reasons for them, and also to agree or disagree with different opinions.

- The examiner may also ask you to reply to your partner's opinions.
- You may want to bring your partner into the discussion, and they might want to involve you in answering their questions, too.
- After you finish Part 4, the examiner will thank you and say the test has ended.

Useful language: opinions

Complete the expressions with these words. In some cases, more than one answer is possible, and you can use some words more than once.

say	opinion	think	feel
hand	feeling	possible	might
views	way	feelings	seems

Asking for someone's opinion

1 What's your ......opinion...... of ...?
2 What do you .... about ...?
3 What are your .... about ...?
4 How do you .... about ...?
5 Could you tell me your .... on ...?

Giving your opinion

6 I ....
7 I'd .... that ...
8 It .... to me ...
9 In my ....
10 My own .... is that ...

Trying to change someone's opinion

11 Yes, but isn't it .... that ...?
12 Yes, but on the other ....
13 But don't you .... that ...?
14 Well, others .... say ...
15 Another .... of looking at it would be ...

Predicting points; listening for expressions

1 Think about the topic of Part 3 (things in the home). Which of points 1–6 do you think the examiner might ask you to discuss? Put a ✓ or a ✗ next to each point. Why are the others unlikely in Part 4?

1 whether houses are too expensive to buy
2 whether everyone in a house should do the same amount of housework
3 how common electrical appliances work
4 whether homes have too much electrical equipment
5 whether you enjoy doing housework
6 which electrical things you have in your house

2 🎧 13 You will hear students Han and Marisol doing Part 4. Decide which of 1–6 is true (T) or false (F) for each person.

		Han	Marisol
1	asks the examiner to repeat the question	F	
2	asks for their partner's opinion		
3	gives reasons for their opinions		
4	gives examples to support their opinions		
5	tries to change their partner's opinion		
6	is polite to the examiner and their partner		

3 🎧 13 Listen again. Tick ✓ the expressions similar to the *Useful language* on the left that Han, Marisol and the examiner use.

Action plan

1 Part 4 questions are not written down, so listen carefully. If you don't understand something, ask the examiner to repeat it (e.g. *I'm sorry, I didn't catch the last word*).

2 Justify your opinions by giving reasons and possibly an example beginning *for instance, for example* or *such as …* .

3 Avoid answers like 'I don't know'. If you don't know a lot about the subject, say so and give your opinion (e.g. *I don't know much about that, but I think …*).

4 Listen carefully to what your partner says, possibly adding to their ideas.

5 Take turns and speak for about the same length of time. If you disagree with your partner's opinions, be polite.

6 Encourage your partner to say more (e.g. *How do you feel about that?* or *What would you do in that situation?*). Then reply.

7 When this part has ended, the Speaking test is over. Remember that the examiners can't answer questions about how well you did.

1 **Think about the topic of Part 3 (restaurants). What issues do you think the examiner might ask you to discuss?**

 Tip! Listen to everything that your partner says and show you are interested in the points that he or she makes.

2 **Work in a group of three if possible. Decide who will be the 'examiner' and who will be the 'candidates'. The examiner should ask the candidates these questions:**

 Tip! Look at the examiner when you are answering his or her questions, but at the other candidate when you are talking together.

| Part 4 | 4 minutes (6 minutes for groups of three) |

Interlocutor Select any of the following questions, as appropriate.

- Do you like to eat in restaurants? Why?/Why not?

- What differences are there between what young people and older people like to eat?

- Do you think we should try to eat food that is produced locally? Why?/Why not?

- Which food or drinks do you think are unhealthy? Why?

- Some people say we eat too much these days. What do you think?

- Which of your country's meals would you miss most if you were abroad? Why?

Select any of the following prompts, as appropriate.

- **What do you think?**
- **Do you agree?**
- **And you?**

Thank you. That is the end of the test.

Test 2 Training Reading and Use of English Part 1

 Page 10 *Task information*

 Page 12 *Action plan*

Useful language: collocations

1 Choose the correct alternative in *italics*.

1 Eating badly can result *on / in* poor health.
2 That old city is known *for / of* its beautiful castle.
3 My teacher is still not satisfied *with / of* my work.
4 Hannah is proud *of / for* her daughter's success.
5 It takes time to get used *to / of* living in another country.
6 The film is based *of / on* events that really happened.
7 I was disappointed *for / with* the food in that café.
8 Leroy is capable *of / in* running 100 metres in under 10 seconds.

2 Add a verb in the correct form to complete the collocations.

1 I .... the last bus home so I had to walk.
2 I'm happy because my team .... yesterday's match 5–0.
3 On Sunday afternoons I often stay at home and .... cards with my family.
4 Please .... this secret. Don't tell anyone.
5 I'll get a car if I .... my driving test.
6 The directors are .... a meeting next week.
7 Last winter I .... a bad cold.
8 Some footballers .... lots of money every week.

> **Tip!** For each gap, look at the whole sentence before you choose the answer.

3 Choose A, B, C or D in these sentences written by First candidates, and say why each is correct.

1 My job involved helping the band to … up their equipment on the stage.
  A put   **B** make   **C** stand   **D** set

2 The sound of the waves makes you sleep … if you were on a cloud.
  A so   **B** just   **C** almost   **D** as

3 I wanted to change the subject, but he … on telling me all the details.
  A suggested   **B** required   **C** insisted   **D** demanded

4 I was woken up in the night by a … noise which came from the first floor.
  A strong   **B** loud   **C** heavy   **D** high

5 As … as I know there were about 5,000 people at the festival.
  A good   **B** far   **C** much   **D** long

6 Unfortunately, our next meeting has been … off until July 1st.
  A left   **B** made   **C** put   **D** turned

7 They both liked the same kind of music and had the same … to life.
  A view   **B** attitude   **C** feeling   **D** opinion

8 Friends can't always agree … everything; each person has her own opinion.
  A on   **B** of   **C** for   **D** in

Advice

1 You need to complete a phrasal verb with 'up' that means 'get everything ready'.

2 Which forms a set phrase with 'if', for something that only seems to be true?

3 Only one of these verbs is followed by 'on'.

4 Which adjective collocates with 'noise'?

5 Which word completes a set phrase meaning 'I think it's true but I'm not sure'?

6 Which option can you add to 'off' to mean 'postpone to a future time'?

7 Only one of these nouns is followed by 'to'.

8 Which preposition follows 'agree' when it means 'have the same opinion about something'?

◄ **Page 12**   *Action plan*

Follow the exam instructions, using the advice to help you.

For questions **1–8**, read the text below and decide which answer (**A**, **B**, **C** or **D**) best fits each gap. There is an example at the beginning (**0**).

Example:

> **Tip!** Understanding the overall meaning of the text makes it easier to choose the correct words for the gaps.

0   **A** keep out of   **B** put up with   **C** miss out on   **D** stand up for

0	A	B	C	D
	☐	■	☐	☐

Planes can make it rain

Living next to an airport has always meant having to **(0)** .... the noise of planes landing and taking off. Now it seems that **(1)** .... residents also have bad weather, according to a **(2)** .... published study.

The scientists looked at satellite **(3)** .... of clouds above airports, and also studied computer models of the way clouds behave. What they found was that as a plane flies through a very cold cloud, the air behind it expands and then cools **(4)** .... rapidly. This sudden drop in temperature, **(5)** .... with the hole formed in the cloud where the plane has passed through, can increase the **(6)** .... of rain or snow on the ground.

In the case of major airports, with hundreds of flights every day, this can have a significant **(7)** .... on weather patterns up to 100 kilometres away. The researchers point out, however, that aircraft passing through clouds are **(8)** .... to affect the global climate.

> **Advice**
>
> **1** Which word goes with 'residents'?
>
> **2** One of these adverbs often goes with 'published'.
>
> **3** Which of these words goes with 'satellite'?
>
> **4** Only one of these adverbs can go with 'rapidly'.
>
> **5** Which is often followed by 'with'?
>
> **6** Which forms a phrase meaning 'to make something more likely'?
>
> **7** Which goes with 'have' and is followed by 'on'?
>
> **8** Which is followed by 'to'?

> **Tip!** Remember to look for prepositions that often follow certain verbs and adjectives.

1	**A** neighbouring	**B** close	**C** local	**D** surrounded
2	**A** lately	**B** recently	**C** lastly	**D** freshly
3	**A** images	**B** figures	**C** aspects	**D** portraits
4	**A** totally	**B** extremely	**C** entirely	**D** perfectly
5	**A** joined	**B** attached	**C** composed	**D** combined
6	**A** forecasts	**B** certainties	**C** chances	**D** opportunities
7	**A** result	**B** influence	**C** consequence	**D** impression
8	**A** doubtful	**B** unsure	**C** unlikely	**D** improbable

◄ **Page 14**   *Task information*

Useful language: relative pronouns, auxiliary verbs and reference words

1   Complete the sentences using each word once.

any	be	despite	did	during
it	round	so	what	whereas

1   This mountain is considered to .... one of the most difficult to climb in the world.
2   Some parents would rather their children .... not have to take so many exams.
3   As he walked onto the stage his mind went blank and he couldn't think .... to say.
4   We enjoyed our day at the beach, ... which we swam several times.
5   I have been intending to do this job for ages, but I just haven't got .... to it yet.
6   The planet Venus is very hot, ... Mars is extremely cold.
7   We needed some more milk, but there wasn't .... left in the fridge.
8   My mother went to that school and .... did I. My daughter will, too.
9   Diamonds and other jewellery are still popular, ... the high prices.
10   I don't think .... makes sense to keep spending so much money.

2   Two of the underlined expressions in these sentences written by First candidates are correct. Correct the eight expressions that are wrong.

1   I still have to finish my project, <u>what</u> keeps me very busy.
2   I really enjoy playing with the computer at your house, because at home I haven't got <u>it</u>.
3   The nurse said, 'Your mother would like to have <u>a</u> word with you,' then she went out.
4   Unfortunately, I cannot attend the meeting <u>owing to</u> I have another appointment.
5   This device can save us money on other costs, <u>although</u> its high purchase price.
6   It was an e-mail from my uncle who lives in Spain, <u>who's</u> name is Enrique.
7   Rose and Damian's engagement has turned out to be a total failure, <u>on account of</u> the fact they have nothing in common.
8   Nowadays there are more and more places <u>when</u> we cannot use our phone.
9   The weather is very cold and the roads are bad because <u>it</u> is a lot of snow.
10   I've chosen two activities, <u>whose</u> are sailing and climbing.

Page 16   *Action plan*

1   Quickly read the article without filling in any gaps. What is the writer's main purpose?

Tip! Remember always to read the whole text before you try to fill in *any* gaps.

2   Follow the exam instructions, using the advice to help you.

For questions **9–16**, read the text below and think of the word which best fits each gap. Use only **one** word in each gap. There is an example at the beginning (0).

Example: | 0 | | O | F | | | | | | | | | | | | | | | | | |

Cycling makes financial sense

These days, most people are aware **(0)** .... the environmental impact of motor vehicles, and they realise that cars are responsible **(9)** .... many of the problems facing their cities. Not **(10)** .... people, however, ever stop **(11)** .... think about how much money they would save by switching from driving to cycling.

Cars cost a lot to buy, and **(12)** .... other major investments such as houses, they quickly lose their value. On **(13)** .... of that, there are running costs such as repair bills, tax and insurance, all of **(14)** .... seem to go up every year.

Bicycles, by contrast, are far **(15)** .... expensive to purchase and maintain, do not require petrol and are easy to park. And if a lot more people took up cycling, the government could spend less of the nation's resources on roads, which at present their taxes help pay for **(16)** .... they drive on them or not.

Advice

9 Which preposition often follows 'responsible'?

10 Complete an expression meaning 'few'.

11 Complete a verb form.

12 You need to make a contrast.

13 Complete an addition link.

14 Which relative pronoun is used for things?

15 Make a contrast with 'costs' that 'go up'.

16 A conjunction is needed.

Tip! Some answers may be auxiliary verbs like *has* or *will*.

Tip! If you can't think of an answer, make the best guess you can. Your answer may be correct.

Page 17 *Task information*

Useful language: word formation

1 Complete the sentences with the correct form of the word in capitals. Look carefully at the words before and after each gap and decide what part of speech you need.

1   I was .... when I heard I had won a holiday in Acapulco!   **DELIGHT**

2   We've got .... coming to our house later this evening.   **VISIT**

3   The .... mountain in Africa is Mount Kilimanjaro, which is 5,895 metres.   **HIGH**

4   In the mountains, it's much .... to travel by horse than by bicycle.   **EASY**

5   Nowadays many people .... travelling by plane and prefer to take the train.   **LIKE**

6   The old house is nearly falling down and it's completely ....   **INHABIT**

7   There are restrictions on car use in a .... number of cities.   **GROW**

8   The most .... countryside here is in the river valley. It's beautiful.   **ATTRACT**

9   Clothes are important in this nightclub and people are always .... dressed.   **FASHION**

10   The owner of that island is extremely .... ; he's worth a billion dollars.   **WEALTH**

2 Correct the mistakes made by First candidates.

1   Thanks for the weekend, everything was wonderfull.

2   Many students study Education and they can find a job eassly when they graduate.

3   I will need at least three days to help my family with the preparatives for this event.

4   The restaurant offers quality, nutritious food, and a variety menu.

5   If we received a complainment from the Tourist Board they would be given the sack immediately.

6   Personally I would recommend this game to unexperienced players who like to solve mysteries.

7   The international airport of the capital city is the most impressing I have ever seen.

8   If you are determined and you focus on your aim, nothing will prevent you from achieving it.

9   Secondly, when I tried to tell your waitress about the food she was rude and unpolite.

10   Car accidents are mainly due to inappropriate speed and uncarefully driving.

Advice

1 'I was' is followed here by an adjective. What form do we use to describe how someone feels?

2 A noun is required, but is it singular or plural? There are two noun forms for this word – which do we need here? ('... coming to our house' should tell you!)

3 An adjective is needed. What form might follow 'the'? The use of a number is a clue.

4 What does 'than' tell you about the missing word? Be careful with the spelling.

5 If they 'prefer' to do something else, is the missing verb likely to be positive or negative? Is a prefix or a suffix required?

6 The missing word describes 'house'. What does 'nearly falling down' tell you about the meaning? You need to add both a prefix and suffix here.

Tip! Remember always to check your spelling!

Page 19   *Action plan*

1   Quickly read the title and the text in the exam task below. What is it about?

2   Look at the example (0) and answer these questions.
- What kind of word is 'predict'?
- What kind of word is needed and what suffix is added to form it?
- What other change is made and why?

3   Follow the exam instructions. For each of 17–24, study the gap, the sentence it is in and the word in capitals.

For questions **17–24**, read the text below. Use the word given in capitals at the end of some of the lines to form a word that fits in the gap **in the same line**. There is an example at the beginning (**0**).

Tip!   When you have filled in all the gaps, read the complete text to make sure everything makes sense.

Tip!   Don't forget you need to make change(s) to ALL the words in capitals. Don't leave any unchanged!

Tip!   Remember to use the context, especially the words next to the gap, to work out what kind of word you need to form (e.g. *noun*, *plural*).

Write your answers **IN CAPITAL LETTERS** on the separate answer sheet.

Example: | 0 | P R E D I C T I O N S |

Too many emails

Some years ago, there were (**0**) .... that email would soon be replaced as the most common means of online communication by social (**17**) .... sites. Since then, however, the number of emails sent has increased (**18**) .... , to the point that the volume received on a daily basis has become (**19**) .... for many people.

For some users, the situation has become so (**20**) .... that they regularly   delete all the emails they receive without even bothering to read them, which is rather (**21**) .... , to say the least. A less extreme measure is to install software that sorts incoming mail into different categories. By doing this, promotions from (**22**) .... organisations, for instance, go into a separate folder from messages arriving from friends or employers, (**23**) .... us to see which emails are more important than others. Not all of us, though, may be so keen to let software make such (**24**) .... for us.

PREDICT

WORK

STEADY

STRESS

BEAR

RISK

COMMERCE

ABLE

DECIDE

Advice

17 Think of a compound word that goes with 'social'.

18 Be careful with the 'y'.

19 Use a word meaning 'something that causes stress'.

20 You need to add both a prefix and a suffix.

21 Make sure you add the correct suffix.

22 Be careful with the final 'e'.

23 A prefix and a suffix are needed, plus a spelling change.

24 Take care with a spelling change.

Page 20   *Task information*

Useful language: reported speech, linking words, conditionals, etc.

1 Complete the second sentence so that it means the same as the first. In each case, underline the words that change in both sentences. (Note: this is not an exam task and there is no key word.)

   1 On Saturday night, I hate staying in by myself.
   On Saturday night, I hate staying in on ....

   2 Despite the fact I was carrying an umbrella, I got completely wet.
   I got completely wet, even ....

   3 Harry is sorry he didn't get up earlier yesterday morning.
   Harry wishes he ....

   4 People believe it was the worst storm in history.
   It is believed to ....

   5 Somebody has painted our house.
   We have had ....

   6 It's years since I swam in the sea.
   I haven't ....

   7 'Are you going to the party?' Ingrid asked me.
   Ingrid asked me ....

   8 I couldn't find Callum's address so I didn't write to him.
   If I hadn't lost Callum's address, I ....

2 Choose the correct words in *italics* in these sentences written by First candidates.

   1 I have wanted to go to India *for / since* years, but never have.
   2 The girl came and asked me if I *will / would* dance with her.
   3 The town was very beautiful, I wish you *were / had been* there to admire its beauty.
   4 The people are really friendly *even if / even though* you don't speak their language.
   5 The local café is said *has / to have* the oldest coffee machine in the country.
   6 I think that you will still have fun *by / on* your own and you will make friends while you are there.
   7 I haven't been to the salon since I *cut my hair / had my hair cut* there six months ago.
   8 *Even so / Even though* the firework display wasn't exciting, I think it was a great event.

Page 22   *Action plan*

1 Study the first sentence in questions 25-30 below. For each sentence, underline the words you think you will have to change. (0) has been done as an example.

2 Follow the exam instructions.

> **Tip!** Don't write the whole sentence on your answer sheet, just the missing words.

> **Tip!** When you've finished, read the first sentence again, then the one you have written. Have you got **all** the ideas from the first sentence in your new sentence?

For questions **25–30**, complete the second sentence so that it has a similar meaning to the first sentence, using the word given. **Do not change the word given.** You must use between **two** and **five** words, including the word given. Here is an example (**0**).

0 Everyone expects that the Olympic champion will win the next race, too.

EXPECTED

The Olympic champion .... win the next race, too.

> **Tip!** Check the number of words you've used. Remember that contracted forms (e.g. *I'm*) count as two words, except *can't* (= *cannot*) which counts as one.

The gap can be filled by the words 'is expected to' so you write:

Example: | **0** | IS EXPECTED TO

Write only the missing words **IN CAPITAL LETTERS on the separate answer sheet.**

---

25 'I'll take you to the station if you're ready,' my brother said.

LONG

My brother said he'd take me to the station .... ready.

26 My bike needs repairing again.

GET

I'll have to .... again.

27 The firm said profits had fallen on account of the recession.

FALL

The firm blamed .... the recession.

28 Sigourney regretted spending so much in the shops.

WISHED

Sigourney .... less in the shops.

29 People believe that poem was written about these beautiful hills.

HAVE

That poem .... written about these beautiful hills.

30 Without your help, I wouldn't have finished the job.

BEEN

I wouldn't have finished the job if .... your help.

> **Advice**
>
> **25** Think of a phrase that can sometimes be used like 'if'.
>
> **26** What structure can we use when someone does something for us?
>
> **27** What preposition sometimes goes with 'blame'?
>
> **28** What verb form often follows the past of 'wish'?
>
> **29** Use two passive verb forms.
>
> **30** Think of a suitable past conditional form.

◀ Page 24 *Task information*

◀ Page 25 *Action plan*

1 Look at the exam instructions below. What kind of text (e.g. *magazine article*) is it?

Tip! Look at A–D *after* you read what the text says. Otherwise you may be misled by the wrong answers.

2 Read the text quickly.
  1 Where is it set?
  2 Who is it mainly about?
  3 What is the main purpose of the text?

3 Follow the exam instructions, using the advice to help you.

You are going to read an article about studying abroad for a year. For questions **31–36** on page 77, choose the answer (**A**, **B**, **C** or **D**) which you think fits best according to the text.

A lot can happen in a year abroad

Like many students before her, studying abroad had a profound affect on Sarah Morrison

As I sat staring out at California's spectacular Big Sur coastline, I felt fortunate to have a sister who had persuaded me to spend a year of my degree abroad. It seems that there are not enough older siblings explaining just how easy it is to take part in an international exchange.

While most universities offer worldwide exchanges, where students swap places with others from all over the world for a semester or a year during their degree, the number and quality on offer, together with the cost and time spent abroad, vary dramatically.

A deciding factor for me in choosing to study at the University of Edinburgh was the fact it offered more than 230 exchange places at overseas universities in the US, Canada, Australia, New Zealand, India, China, South Korea, Japan, Singapore and South America.

Despite all this choice, I still found that deciding to spend a year abroad was something of a novelty, with most of my friends giving more thought to embracing Edinburgh than packing their bags to leave a city that had only just become their home. Yet, fortified by my sister's advice and a Californian friend who told me I would love the coast, I applied to spend my third year at the University of

California, Berkeley – never guessing that this would affect almost every future decision I would make.

From the start of your exchange, you are aware that the time you have in your new country is limited and not to be wasted. Your experience is shaped by a predetermined start and end, which immediately increases the significance of the time in between.

From the first week I arrived, I started to work at *The Daily Californian,* Berkeley's student newspaper. I moved from an international house with more than 600 students from all over the world into a co-operative house where 60 of us shared responsibility for management of the building. I met people from Calcutta, Cairo and Chile, and learnt that holding on to any stereotypes I might have about Americans would be about as useful as assuming that all European people lived on farms.

The grades I earned at Berkeley didn't actually count towards my degree classification at Edinburgh. However, I studied under a Pulitzer Prize-winning poet, signed up for student-led seminars and took an African American literature class that shaped my dissertation in Edinburgh. Whether I was learning about contemporary poets on a tour of San Francisco or reporting on the President's speech in San Francisco for the next day's newspaper, my stay there enabled me to return to Edinburgh with an increased sense of awareness about what I wanted to gain from my English literature degree.

While the expense might seem like an initial barrier to international exchanges, in reality they can actually save a student money. Visas, health insurance and flights to the chosen country will have to be bought, but a student will usually only be charged 25 to 50 per cent of their home university's annual fees. A student travelling abroad is entitled to a larger student loan, and grants are available at many institutions for students going on an exchange.

Taking part in an exchange may not appeal to all students. You have to research the options independently, apply almost a year before you go away and be aware of the grades required in the first year to qualify for a place on one. Even so, Edinburgh's international exchange officer, Helen Leitch, says: 'If I had a pound for every time that students told me it was the best experience of their life, I would be a very wealthy woman indeed.'

line 64

31 One reason Sarah became a student at Edinburgh University was that
   A she could first study abroad and then move to Edinburgh.
   B her sister had previously studied at Edinburgh.
   C she could do part of her studies at a suitable university abroad.
   D most of the students at Edinburgh spend a year at an overseas university.

> **Tip!** Underline the key words in the stem. Then look for expressions in the text that mean the same or the opposite.

32 How did Sarah feel when she went to Berkeley?
   A She was pleased to find the people were exactly as she had expected.
   B She knew she wanted to make the most of her stay there.
   C She wanted to get a job rather than begin studying immediately.
   D She began to wish her stay there could be a little shorter.

33 What does Sarah feel she achieved at Berkeley?
   A She formed a clearer idea of what her long-term aims were.
   B She took the first steps towards becoming a teacher.
   C She developed her poetry-writing skills significantly.
   D She ensured that she would graduate with a first-class degree.

34 What does Sarah say about the cost of an international university exchange?
   A As a student you can get reduced rates for health insurance.
   B Your fees may be cut by half for every year of your course.
   C It can be cheaper overall than studying in your own country.
   D Taking cheap flights abroad can save you a lot of money.

35 What does 'one' refer to in line 64?
   A an international exchange as part of a university course
   B a research degree at a university in another country
   C a university course that is paid for by the government
   D the first year of a university course in your own country

36 What does Helen Leitch suggest in the final paragraph?
   A Students who do international exchanges often go on to become extremely rich.
   B Most students who've done an international exchange believe it was highly worthwhile.
   C Only students from rich families can afford to do an international exchange.
   D She should be paid a far higher salary for organising international exchanges.

> **Advice**
>
> *31 Look for an expression that means 'one reason'.*
>
> *32 Look for her thoughts on how students feel when they begin their stay abroad.*
>
> *33 Focus on her feelings after she had left Berkeley.*
>
> *34 Study the next-to-last paragraph after 'international exchanges'.*
>
> *35 Find the countable noun that it refers back to.*
>
> *36 Is she really talking about money, or using an idiom?*

Page 28 *Task information*

Page 29 *Action plan*

1 Look at the exam instructions, the title and the introduction to the text in *italics* below. What kind of text (e.g. *fiction*, *advertisement*) is it?

Tip! After you fill in all the gaps, read through the completed text. Can you see the links in ideas and language between the main text and the sentences from A–G?

2 Follow the exam instructions, using the advice to help you.

You are going to read an article in which a television news producer talks about his work. Six sentences have been removed from the article. Choose from the sentences **A–G** on page 79 the one which fits each gap (**37–42**). There is one extra sentence which you do not need to use.

Working as a TV news producer

Rob Cole has produced TV news for decades now, working on anything from international celebrities to global conflicts. He shares the benefit of his considerable experience in the industry

Rob's time behind the cameras has coincided with huge changes in the way news is reported – from a time when everyone bought local newspapers, through the birth of 24-hour rolling news, and now the Internet. But what is the work like on a day-to-day basis?

Rob's always worked in foreign news, so his focus is obviously on news from around the world. As you can imagine, there's a lot of that. Rob comes in early, having checked his phone, social media, and listened to as many news programmes as he could. **37** Running the foreign section is like a never-ending contest – constantly trying to get his journalists' news presented ahead of the TV station's other sections.

Once you have a story it's then a matter of making sure that wherever the journalist is, the report comes into the building – through satellite, Internet or other routes – and it is ready to run on air on time. **38** There's nothing like getting a note from the producer at another network congratulating on a job well done. The low points, on the other hand, are much less pleasant: 'I've had colleagues badly injured.'

So how can you become a news producer? Says Rob: 'We get loads of applications. **39** Don't be put off; people in this business admire people who don't give up easily, for obvious reasons.'

You need to be keen to learn and, of course, take a real interest in current affairs. 'You have to be obsessed with news, constantly following it. Even if you're a creative producer, doing graphics, you still have to care about what's going on in the world. Also, some people think about going into the media just because it sounds exciting. That would be a mistake; you have to really want to do the job. Luck's involved too, of course. **40** '.

In some ways, Rob's job should remain fairly constant for the next few years. 'They will always need someone to make decisions and take responsibility for newsgathering. However, what will change is the way in which news is delivered. When I started in TV, the crew used to consist of a reporter, producer, a camera operator, a sound person, and sometimes even a separate lighting person. **41** Now there's just the reporter and a multitasking camera operator who also edits and supplies the written material – if you're lucky!'

'Before long there will be a crew of just one, shooting all their own material on a smartphone, then editing and voicing that material, before sending it to head office, where it ends up going straight on air. **42** Actually, this has already started to happen. The technology will just get quicker and quicker and smaller and smaller.'

A You might write to just the right person at the right time.

B Turning the device around and pressing the live app button also enables live broadcasting into the same programme.

C They would be loaded down with equipment and some of them would be linked by cable.

D With this information, before any stories actually come in, he then decides on the news priorities of the day.

E In those days it was possible to start a career in news without even going to university: you went straight into training on a local paper.

F Making sure it does so matters, especially given the friendly competition with other TV networks: 'beating the other networks' is a real highlight.

G I always endeavour to reply, but from my own experience too many people don't get back to you, so it's best to keep trying.

Tip! Each time you choose one of A–G, cross it out so that you don't have to keep reading through the whole list. This will save you time.

Tip! Underline reference and linking expressions, vocabulary links and words that avoid repetition in both the main text and sentences A–G.

Advice

37 Look for a sentence that focuses on planning early in the morning.

38 Which sentence says it is important that the story goes out on time?

39 Look for an expression that means 'don't give up easily'.

40 Which sentence suggests you could have good 'luck'?

41 Look for a verb form sometimes used in a similar way to 'used to'.

42 What kind of thing is a 'smartphone'?

Page 31   *Task information*

Page 32   *Action plan*

1   Look at the exam instructions below and the title and layout of the text on page 81.

    1   What kind of text is it? How many parts is it in?

    2   What is the topic? Who are the people?

    3   What kind of information must you find?

2   Follow the exam instructions, using the advice to help you.

You are going to read a magazine article about adults who have met an old school friend again through social media. For questions **43–52**, choose from the people (**A–E**). The people may be chosen more than once.

Which person

is surprised at the job her friend now has?	**43**
is sure that this time their friendship will last?	**44**
thinks her life may have changed as a result of meeting her friend again?	**45**
feels that in one way she and her friend have similar personalities?	**46**
believes that even without the Internet they would have met again?	**47**
regrets losing contact with her friend years ago?	**48**
was initially unsure whether she wanted to talk to her friend again?	**49**
told her friend she was sad to hear what had happened to her?	**50**
was surprised at how little her friend's appearance had changed?	**51**
admits she wrongly predicted her friend would never have a successful career?	**52**

Advice

43 Look for a contrast with the person's skills at school.

44 Be careful: one person seems to say this, but eventually says the opposite.

45 Look for a comparative form indicating change.

46 Look for a phrase that means 'similar'.

47 Look for a way of expressing certainty in the past.

48 Which past modal form can express regret?

49 Look for words that mean 'initially' and 'unsure'.

50 Think of another way of saying 'I told her I was sad to hear'.

51 Look for a different way of saying how little she had changed.

52 Look for a contrast, and an admission she was wrong.

Friends again

Five people talk about the school friends they have met up with again thanks to social media websites.

A Nadia Hassan

Although we've been living in different countries for a long time, I know I should have made more of an effort to stay in touch with Amina because we always got on well together, even though we're quite different people. For instance, I'm much more ambitious than her and have no plans to start a family, whereas she already has two children. It's quite a contrast in lifestyle, and although it's great that we're both content with our own lives – and we've enjoyed catching up with each other's news – I don't really know whether in the future we'll have enough in common to keep the relationship going.

B Julia Nowak

The first thing that struck me was that Natalia still looked much the same as she had ten years earlier, unlike some other people in their late twenties – especially those who have had serious personal issues to deal with during that time. She's also still very keen on sports, which I'm not, but she remains as sociable as she ever was and I suppose we're quite alike in that respect. In fact, she was one of the first people I thought of when the idea of contacting my old classmates occurred to me, and it's great you can do that online so easily. Otherwise you could lose touch with them forever.

C Olivia Morgan

Back in our school days I always liked Megan, but she was never keen on studying so I sort of took it for granted that she would end up doing a job that didn't require qualifications. Now it turns out she went on to do really well academically and for two years was a Philosophy lecturer at a top university. The other mistake I made was being rather cautious about responding when she first got in touch with me online last autumn, when in fact as soon as we saw each other on the screen we started chatting again as if that ten-year gap had never existed. I think we both quickly realised that we wouldn't ever let anything like that happen again.

D Maite Silva

I was delighted when Carla told me she has such a good job. Somehow I always knew she'd do well, though I must confess that back then she was the last person I would have imagined becoming an economist because she was pretty hopeless at maths. But when she appeared on my laptop screen after all those years I was impressed by how mature she sounded and looked, and in fact she might be having an influence on me. Ever since we met up again, I've found myself taking a more serious attitude to my career, with promotion now a real possibility.

E Yan Lin

When I realised my old classmate Ming was trying to contact me I didn't hesitate for a second in replying. Somehow I'd always known that one way or another we were bound to run into each other at some point, because when we left school we'd both gone off to do the same subject at different universities. What I hadn't been prepared for, though, was the news that she'd had to interrupt her studies owing to personal problems. I expressed my sympathy, but she assured me she'd recovered and eventually graduated, and that since then she's been working in advertising. Which of course is exactly what I do, too.

> **Tip!** When you are reading the text to find evidence, look for the same meanings as the questions, not the same words.

> **Tip!** Remember that there may be parts of the text that are not tested.

◀ **Page 34**   *Task information*

Understanding the task; ordering points or reasons; adding information

1 Fill in the gaps in this text about Writing Part 1, using each item from the box once.

against	both	each	formal	idea	linking
notes	opinion	own	plan	range	140

In Writing Part 1, you write an essay giving your **(1)** .... on a particular topic in at least **(2)** .... words. You are given two very brief **(3)** .... to guide your writing, and you also have to add an **(4)** .... of your own. You can choose to write for or **(5)** .... the statement or question that forms the topic, or else give arguments on **(6)** .... sides, followed by your **(7)** .... opinion in the conclusion. As your essay is for a teacher, you should write in a fairly **(8)** .... style, using a variety of **(9)** .... expressions such as *Firstly*. You need to be careful with grammar, spelling and punctuation, and try to use a wide **(10)** .... of words, phrases and structures. You should always make a **(11)** .... for your text before you start writing, listing the points you are going to mention about **(12)** .... of the three notes.

2 With your partner, if you have one, think of two linking expressions for each of 1–4.

1 to make the first point   3 to make the last point
2 to make more points   4 to introduce the conclusion

3 Which of these linking expressions can be used at the beginning of a sentence, followed by a comma? Which cannot?

also   as well   as well as that   besides   furthermore   in addition   too

4a Look at this Writing Part 1 exam task and answer the questions.

1 What is the topic of the essay?   2 Which two points must you discuss?

In your English class you have been talking about the problems of 21st-century urban living. Now your English teacher has asked you to write an essay.

Write an essay using all the notes and give reasons for your point of view.

Cars should be banned from city centres.

Notes

Write about:

1 noise and pollution

2 transport

3 .... (your own idea)

b Now read the model essay below, ignoring the gaps for now, and answer the questions.

1 Does the writer argue for or against the statement, or give arguments on both sides?

2 In which paragraph does the writer discuss each of notes 1 and 2?

3 Which other main point does the writer discuss, and where?

4 What is the writer's opinion and where is it stated?

c Fill in gaps 1–8 with suitable linking expressions. In most cases more than one answer is possible.

In cities everywhere, there is growing concern about the effect of motor vehicles on the inhabitants' quality of life. Some people want to prohibit cars from urban areas, and to a great extent I agree.

(1) ...., these vehicles poison the air with their exhaust fumes, contributing to the clouds of smog that hang over many cities, especially in sunny weather. (2) ...., the sounds of engines and car horns destroys the peace of our neighbourhoods, even at night.

(3) ...., the huge amount of traffic nowadays makes cities less pleasant places to live. For instance, crossing busy roads often takes ages. (4) ...., they can be dangerous, especially for children, and for old or disabled people, (5) ....

(6) ...., there are often alternatives to travelling by car, such as the tube, buses or trams. (7) ...., if there were no cars, far more people would cycle to work, or they could walk there in the fresh air.

(8) ...., urban areas without cars would be much better places to live. As long as other means of transport are available, therefore, I believe our cities should become totally car-free.

◄ **Page 37** *Action plan*

1 Look at the exam instructions below.

   1 What do you have to write about?

   2 Who is your essay for?

   3 Which two main points must you include?

You **must** answer this question. Write your answer in **140–190** words in an appropriate style.

In your English class you have been talking about the effects of rising living standards on the environment. Now your English teacher has asked you to write an essay.

Write an essay using all the notes and give reasons for your point of view.

Which is more important: improving people's standard of living or protecting the environment?

Notes

Write about:

   1 employment

   2 housing

   3 .... (your own idea)

---

2 Do the exam task.

Tip! Use expressions such as *firstly* and *besides* to link points together to form a complete text.

Tip! Introduce your own opinion with a suitable expression such as *I believe (that)* ... or *In my view* ... .

Tip! When you've finished, check you've included all three notes and have given appropriate answers. And don't forget to allow time to check your essay for mistakes.

Page 38 *Writing Part 2 information*

Task information

- The letter task in Part 2 tests your ability to write, for example, a formal job application or a letter to a magazine editor. You must write in an appropriate style.
- The instructions include a description of a situation. In response to this situation, you have to write a letter of between 140–190 words.

- You should allow about 40 minutes for this task, including time at the end to check your work.
- You have to organise your text into paragraphs, with a suitable beginning and ending.
- You should write full sentences with correct grammar and punctuation, using a good range of language with accurate spelling.

Useful language: formal expressions

Complete the formal expressions with the words given.

1 Giving a reason for writing

> writing   reply   apply   saw

- a **I recently** .... **your advertisement in** the newspaper.
- b **I would like to** .... **for** the position of trainee chef.
- c **I am** .... **to inform you** of a serious incident.
- d **In** .... **to your recent letter, I would like to** make two points.

2 Describing yourself

> suitable   experience   good   knowledge

- a **I have had some** .... **of** this kind of work.
- b **I am particularly** .... **at** solving problems.
- c **I feel I would be** .... **for** the job as I have the right skills.
- d **I have a good** .... **of** information technology.

3 Complaining

> complain   pleased   disappointed   complaint

- a **I was extremely** .... **with** the item I bought.
- b **I am writing to** .... **about** the service in your shop.
- c **I wish to make a** .... **about** the delay in delivery.
- d **I am not at all** .... **about** the reply I received.

4 Requesting action

> please   like   grateful   must

- a **I would be most** .... **if you could** send me an application form.
- b **Would you** .... **ensure** that this does not happen again.
- c **I feel I** .... **ask you to** make a formal written apology.
- d **I would therefore** .... **you to** investigate this matter.

Text layout; formal & informal language; error correction

1 Look at the exam instructions below.

1 What is the situation?
2 What did you expect from your evening at the theatre?
3 Should you write in a formal or informal style?

You recently attended this event at a city-centre theatre, but you did not enjoy it.

> **The perfect evening out!**
>
> - Top-class musical entertainment, with famous artists
> - Excellent restaurant
> - Discounts available for young people

Write a letter of complaint to the manager, saying what went wrong.

2 ⊙ Look at this letter written by a First candidate. Find and correct the following (1–3):

1 poor layout. Where should it be divided into paragraphs?
2 two informal expressions, four contracted forms and four uses of informal punctuation. Change these to more formal language.

3 two mistakes each in verb forms, spelling and capital letters. Correct these.

Dear sir,

I'm writing to you to complain about the musical last night. I was looking forward to seeing your show but I have to say that it was a very disapointing evening. Firstly, my favourite singer Carmen Sánchez didn't perform, without any explanation being given. In addition, the show should started at 19.30 as it said in the newspaper, not 20.15! I was sure that discounts were available because I have read that they were, but the tickets office didn't offer them. So I had to pay full price for the ticket. What a terrible shock! After the show I was hungry so I went upstairs to the restaurant, but I was very surprised to find it was closed!

I hope you understand how I feel about this. It certainly wasn't a perfect evening out so I want to have my money back!

Yours Faithfully,

Emilio Ricci

3 ⊙ Study the exam instructions below and the model letter written by Felipe, a very strong First candidate.

1 Is Felipe's letter the right length, and written in a suitable style?
2 Where does he deal with the three points in the advertisement?
3 What else does he say about himself?
4 What has he sent with his letter? Why?
5 What does he suggest to the employer?

You have seen this advertisement in an English-language newspaper.

CHILLI PEPPER CAFÉ
Waiter/Waitress required

The person we are looking for will be:
- good with people
- prepared to work long hours
- experienced in this kind of work

Apply to the manager, Ms Harrison, saying why you are suitable for a job at our café.

Write your **letter of application**.

Tip! You don't have to write any postal or email addresses in either letter or email tasks.

Letter begins Dear Ms ...

Dear Ms Harrison,

I wish to apply for the post of waiter at the Chilli Pepper Café, as advertised in the newspaper on October 22. → *Say where you saw the ad*

Correct structure for current job →

For the past two years I have been working at McDonald's and there I have gained wide experience in dealing with people. Cooking is the only hobby I have, and so I am very interested in different kinds of food. In view of the fact that I am used to working long hours, I believe I am ideally suited for this job. → *Formal linking expressions*

Another reason for applying is that your café is only five minutes away from my home. Consequently, I would have only a short distance to travel every day. → *Don't use 'will' until you get the job!*

I enclose a copy of my curriculum vitae, which will give you further details of my career to date.

Be polite to the employer →

I hope this information will be sufficient for you to consider my application. If you need further details, please do not hesitate to contact me. For an interview I could make myself available at any time. → *Be helpful*

I look forward to hearing from you.

Yours sincerely,

Felipe Martin

Action plan

1 Study the exam instructions below and the situation. Think about who you have to write to, why, and which points to include. Should you use formal or informal language?

2 Make a plan and write down all your ideas. How many paragraphs will you need?

3 Put your best ideas under paragraph headings. Also note down some words and phrases for each paragraph, including expressions from *Useful language* on pages 38 and 39.

4 Write your text, keeping to the topic and to your plan. Use a wide range of vocabulary and grammar, and make sure your handwriting is easy to read.

5 Leave enough time at the end to check for mistakes – and that you have written at least 140 words.

Tip! Always put the opening (e.g. *Dear Frankie* or *Dear Mr Williams*), the closing (e.g. *Best wishes* or *Yours sincerely*) and your own name on separate lines. Never begin *Dear Manager* or *Dear Friend* – use their name.

Tip! If you begin your letter *Dear Sir* or *Dear Madam*, end it *Yours faithfully*; if you use the person's surname, e.g. *Dear Ms Kay*, end with *Yours sincerely*.

1 Look at the exam instructions below.

    1 What do you have to read?

    2 What kind of job is it?

    3 Which points must you deal with?

    4 What style should you write in?

You see this advertisement in an English language magazine.

Temporary staff required

Holiday jobs with Countryside Camps

We are looking for people to work at one of our exciting camps in the heart of the countryside this summer.

Do you enjoy working with young people? Do you like sports? Do you speak English and at least one other language?

If so, apply in writing to: Paul Taylor, Countryside Camps.

Write your **letter of application**.

2 Study the exam question and write your answer in 140–190 words in an appropriate style.

Task information (review)

- The review task in Part 2 tests your ability to describe something you have experienced (e.g. a TV programme or a product) and give your opinion of it, with a recommendation to the reader.
- You read a description of a situation and then write a review of it in **140–190** words. You should allow about 40 minutes for this task, including time at the end to check your work.
- The instructions also tell you where your review will be published (e.g. in a student newsletter). You therefore have to write in an appropriate style.
- You need to organise your text into paragraphs.
- You should write full sentences and try to use correct grammar, punctuation and spelling and a good range of language.

Useful language: review

1 Match the headings in the box with the groups of expressions 1–4.

| Advising not to do something   Recommending   Criticising   Praising |

1 ....

It was one of the best ... I have ever ...

The ... was absolutely perfect, and ...

We had (a pleasant/an enjoyable/a marvellous, etc.) time at ...

I was pleased to see that ...

It was a nice surprise to find that ...

... was even better than we had expected

2 ....

There should have been ...

I thought there was going to be ... but there was only ...

The advertisement said that ... but in fact ...

We were (rather) disappointed to find that ...

There weren't enough ... to ... / it was too ... to ...

There wasn't any ... at all

3 ....

Anyone who likes ... will really enjoy ...

Don't miss the opportunity to ...

I'm sure everyone will find ... worth (listening to/visiting/trying, etc.).

If you get the chance to ... (see it/buy one/go there, etc.), ... I would advise ...

4 ....

I (would strongly) advise against (watching/reading/eating, etc.) this ...

My advice is to avoid this ... and ... instead.

I (would) suggest finding a better ... than this, such as ...

2 Complete the sentences with contrast links. Use each word once.

| spite   even   despite   although   however |

1 ..... the concert started on time, it finished early.

2 It rained every day. ..... this, we all enjoyed our holiday.

3 The theme park has some excellent rides. ..... , the queues were very long.

4 It's a good film, in ..... of the poor acting at times.

5 I would certainly read this book again, ... though it is 800 pages long.

3 Rewrite 1–5 so that the second sentence means the same as the first.

1 It was late at night, but the club was still empty. ⟶ The club was still empty, even _____

2 The traffic was heavy, but we arrived on time. ⟶ In spite _____

3 We asked twice for coffee, but the waiter didn't bring it. ⟶ Although _____

4 We were a long way from the stage, but I could see the band on the screens. ⟶ Even _____

5 The bed was too short, but I would still recommend this hotel. ⟶ Despite _____

Understanding instructions

1 Study the exam instructions below and underline the key words.

1 What situation do you have to think about?

2 Who are you going to write a review for? What style of writing is suitable?

3 What two things do the instructions say you must do?

4 What else should you add?

You see this notice on a travel website.

> **Reviews wanted!**
>
> What did you think of the last holiday home you stayed in? Write a review of a house or apartment anywhere in the world for our popular website for travellers and tourists. Describe the holiday home and say why you did or did not enjoy your stay there.
>
> Interesting reviews will appear on our site within 24 hours.

Write your **review** in 140–190 words in an appropriate style.

2 Quickly read the model review below. Did the writer enjoy staying in the apartment?

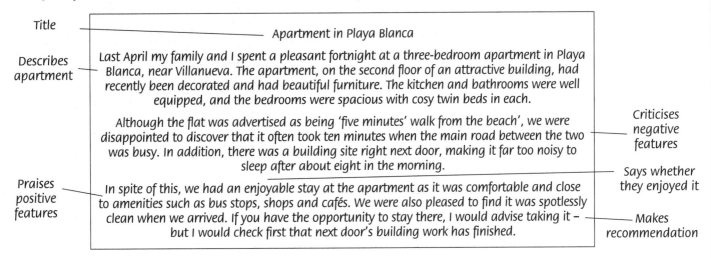

Title —

Describes apartment —

Apartment in Playa Blanca

Last April my family and I spent a pleasant fortnight at a three-bedroom apartment in Playa Blanca, near Villanueva. The apartment, on the second floor of an attractive building, had recently been decorated and had beautiful furniture. The kitchen and bathrooms were well equipped, and the bedrooms were spacious with cosy twin beds in each.

Although the flat was advertised as being 'five minutes' walk from the beach', we were disappointed to discover that it often took ten minutes when the main road between the two was busy. In addition, there was a building site right next door, making it far too noisy to sleep after about eight in the morning.

Praises positive features —

In spite of this, we had an enjoyable stay at the apartment as it was comfortable and close to amenities such as bus stops, shops and cafés. We were also pleased to find it was spotlessly clean when we arrived. If you have the opportunity to stay there, I would advise taking it – but I would check first that next door's building work has finished.

— Criticises negative features

— Says whether they enjoyed it

— Makes recommendation

3 Study the text and the notes more carefully.

1 What reasons does the writer give for enjoying being there? What advice does he/she give?

2 What adjectives (words and phrases) describe the apartment and the building?

3 Which contrast links are used? Which other linking expressions can you find?

4 Which expressions similar to those in *Useful language* on page 88 does the writer use (e.g. *spent a pleasant fortnight at …*)?

> **Tip!** Before you plan your review, decide whether you enjoyed yourself or not.

Action plan

1 Read the instructions and try to think of something relevant that you have seen, heard or read to review. Or just use your imagination.

2 Think about who the readers of your review will be and what they will want to know.

3 Note down some points to mention, and spend a few minutes making a plan that includes a description, an explanation and a recommendation. Decide how many paragraphs you will use.

4 Give your review a title that tells readers what it is about.

5 Write your text in a style that is appropriate for the publication and the readers.

6 Use some of the expressions from *Useful language* on page 88 to praise, criticise, advise or recommend.

7 Use some of the contrast links on page 88 to describe unexpected things, or to make both positive and negative points.

8 Finish by recommending or advising readers against the subject of your review (e.g. *it would make the perfect day out for young people*).

1　Read the exam task below.

　　1　Who is your review for?

　　2　What three things do you have to do?

You see this announcement in the English-language magazine of your college.

Restaurant reviews wanted

Classes sometimes like to celebrate special occasions by going out for a meal together. Write a review of a suitable restaurant that you like. Describe the atmosphere and the food, and explain why you think your class would enjoy being there.

The three best reviews will be published in the next issue of the magazine.

2　Write your **review** in 140–190 words in an appropriate style.

Tip! Try to include some interesting facts and lively comments in your review.

Page 43   *Task information*

Understanding the task

1   Complete the text about writing articles, using each word from the box once.

> ending   experiences   informal   interest   introduction
> magazine   opinions   strong   title   topic

Before you choose the article task in Writing Part 2, be sure you know enough about the **(1)** .... to write 140–190 words about it. You will usually be asked to write for a newsletter or **(2)** .... , and your readers will have the same **(3)** .... as you, for example a hobby or type of music. To catch their attention, you should think of a good, short **(4)** .... , and then write an interesting **(5)** .... in the first paragraph to keep them reading. You can write your text in quite an **(6)** .... style, using some **(7)** .... , colourful adjectives and expressing your own **(8)** .... You can also include descriptions of your own **(9)** .... and ensure that the **(10)** .... of the article is particularly interesting by making your readers think about what they have just read.

Useful language: strong expressions

2   Match the strong expressions in *italics* with the adjectives in the box.

> beautiful   clean   crowded   hot   hungry   old   small   surprising   tasty   unhappy

1 The ice-cream desserts are even more *delicious* than they look on the menu.
2 If the air-conditioning on the Metro breaks down, it gets *boiling* down there.
3 From the top of the skyscraper, the vehicles far below look *tiny*.
4 In spring there are *gorgeous* wild flowers in a whole range of colours.
5 It is *astonishing* how few people visit such a magnificent old building.

6 The people looked *miserable* as they stood in the rain waiting for buses that never came.
7 Further up the hill are the remains of *ancient* walls that once protected the town.
8 After a full day's skiing without a break for lunch, we were *starving*.
9 The living room was tidy and the bathroom was absolutely *spotless*.
10 The stadium is always *packed* when local teams play each other.

3   Use each of the words in italics in a sentence of your own.

Understanding instructions

1   Study the exam instructions below and underline the key words.

1 Who has asked you to write the article?
2 What will happen if you write one of the best articles?

You see this announcement in your college newsletter.

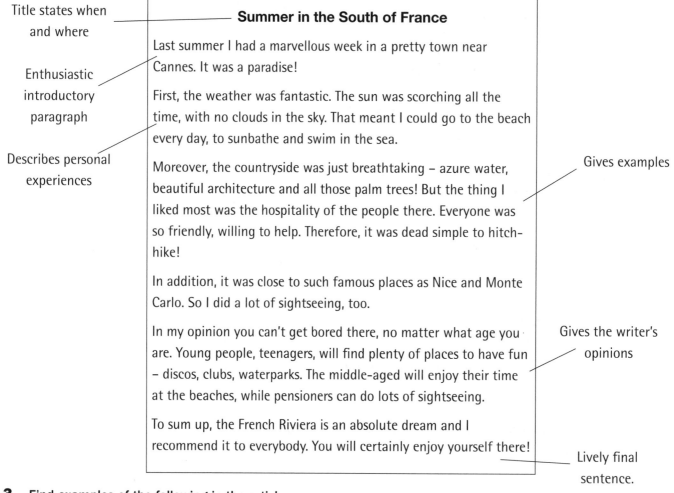

Travel articles wanted

Have you been somewhere recently that you really liked? If so, write an article describing the place and explaining why you would recommend it to other people.

The best articles will be published in the next month's Newsletter.

Write your **article** in 140–190 words in an appropriate style.

2 Quickly read this strong First candidate's article and the notes next to it.
  1 Is the text well organised into paragraphs?
  2 Is it written in an appropriate style?
  3 Does it deal with both parts of the task? If so, where?

Title states when and where

Enthusiastic introductory paragraph

Describes personal experiences

Summer in the South of France

Last summer I had a marvellous week in a pretty town near Cannes. It was a paradise!

First, the weather was fantastic. The sun was scorching all the time, with no clouds in the sky. That meant I could go to the beach every day, to sunbathe and swim in the sea.

Moreover, the countryside was just breathtaking – azure water, beautiful architecture and all those palm trees! But the thing I liked most was the hospitality of the people there. Everyone was so friendly, willing to help. Therefore, it was dead simple to hitch-hike!

In addition, it was close to such famous places as Nice and Monte Carlo. So I did a lot of sightseeing, too.

In my opinion you can't get bored there, no matter what age you are. Young people, teenagers, will find plenty of places to have fun – discos, clubs, waterparks. The middle-aged will enjoy their time at the beaches, while pensioners can do lots of sightseeing.

To sum up, the French Riviera is an absolute dream and I recommend it to everybody. You will certainly enjoy yourself there!

Gives examples

Gives the writer's opinions

Lively final sentence.

3 Find examples of the following in the article.
  1 addition links
  2 result links
  3 strong expressions, including adjectives and phrases
  4 informal language

◀ Page 46   *Action plan*

1   Read the exam task below.

    1   Who are you writing for?

    2   Which two things must you write about?

You see this announcement in an online magazine.

> **Articles wanted**
>
> ### Health and fitness
>
> In today's world, how can we remain healthy? How can we keep ourselves fit?
>
> Write us an article answering these questions.
>
> The best articles will appear on our website within a week.

2   Write your **article** in 140–190 words in an appropriate style.

Tip! Try to use a wide variety of grammatical structures in your answer.

Page 50   *Task information*

 Page 51   *Action plan*

1   Read the first two lines of questions 1–8 below. For each one, answer these questions where possible.

   1   What is the situation?

   2   Will you hear one female, one male, or two speakers?

> **Tip!** Read the question and try to imagine the situation. Who's talking to whom? Where? Why? When? How do they feel?

2   What is the focus of the question in the second line?
Example: question 1: language function

> **Tip!** Remember that you can change your mind about an answer while you listen for the first or the second time.

3   🎧 **14** Follow the exam instructions, using the advice to help you.

You will hear people talking in eight different situations. For questions **1–8**, choose the best answer (**A**, **B** or **C**).

---

1   You hear part of a conversation in a watch repair shop.
What is the man doing?
   A   refusing to accept the watch for repair
   B   encouraging the customer to buy a watch
   C   advising the customer to have the watch mended elsewhere

2   You are on a train and you hear a woman leaving a message on an answering machine.
Why is she calling?
   A   to arrange a lift from the station
   B   to change the time of her evening meal
   C   to find out bus times from the station

3   You hear a talent show judge commenting on a performance she has just seen.
What does she think of the man's performance?
   A   He lacks confidence.
   B   He chose the wrong song.
   C   He has a weak singing voice.

4   You hear the beginning of a talk in a community centre.
What will the talk be about?
   A   local history
   B   transport problems
   C   modern agriculture

Advice

1 Always listen to the end before choosing an answer.

2 Listen for an expression used to ask someone a favour.

3 Focus on the speaker's own opinion, not that of other people.

4 Concentrate on the main subject, not other matters the speaker may mention.

5 Think of words for the main parts of A–C, and phrasal verbs often used with each.

6 Which other structure might be used for each of A–C?

7 Listen for what they agree they like, not what they dislike.

8 Listen for reasons why two of A–C are wrong.

5 You hear a man talking about saving money.

He wants to buy

A a motorcycle.

B a bicycle.

C a car.

6 You hear a woman talking about a concert being cancelled.

What does she think about this?

A She is glad it will not take place.

B It should be re-arranged for a later date.

C She should have been told sooner.

7 You hear a man and woman talking about a flat they are considering renting.

What do they both like about it?

A the size

B the low rent

C the furniture

8 You hear a woman talking about her tablet computer.

How does she feel about it?

A She finds something about it annoying.

B She wants to get a more powerful model.

C She spends too much time using it.

Page 53 *Task information*

Page 54 *Action plan*

1   Read the exam instructions below.

  1   What kind of recording (e.g. *a talk*) is it?

  2   What's the topic?

  3   Who will you hear?

  4   For each gap, what kind of information (e.g. *a verb*, *a day of the week*) do you need to listen for?

Tip! Only write one answer, even if you can think of two or more good ones.

Tip! There is always plenty of time between each answer for you to write down the missing words.

2   🎧 15 Follow the exam instructions, using the advice to help you. **[You will need to play this recording twice.]**

You will hear a man called Markus Fischer talking about mooncake, a traditional Asian bakery product. For questions **9–18**, complete the sentences with a word or short phrase.

Mooncake

Markus was staying in **(9)** .... when he first tried mooncake.

Markus's favourite kind of mooncake has a filling made of **(10)** ....

Markus says that he likes to have **(11)** .... with mooncake.

Mooncake is popular during the Moon Festival, which last year was held in **(12)** ....

The mooncake Marcus was given during the festival had the shape of a **(13)** .... on the top.

Markus was surprised to learn that mooncake is rarely made **(14)** .... in China.

The people Markus was staying with received mooncake from their **(15)** ....

His host family gave Markus a mooncake that had a slightly **(16)** .... flavour.

Markus was told that, many years ago, people used mooncakes to send **(17)** .... to each other.

After people had read what was written on the mooncake, they **(18)** .... it.

Tip! Underline the key words in each question, then listen for words and phrases that express the same idea.

Tip! Write clearly, so that you can read your answers later and copy them correctly onto the answer sheet.

Tip! Check your answers are grammatically correct (e.g. singular/plural, verb tense).

Advice

9 Be careful – you will hear a number of place names.

10 He mentions a variety of fillings. Listen carefully for the correct one.

11 Listen for an expression that means 'with'.

12 You need last year's month, not other years.

13 Take care when other designs on mooncakes are mentioned.

14 Listen for something he expected to be the case, but was not.

15 Be careful – different kinds of people are mentioned.

16 Make sure you don't choose the wrong flavour.

17 Think of another way of saying 'send'.

18 Focus on what was written on top of the cake, not inside it.

Page 55   *Task information*

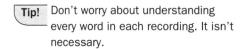 **Page 56**   *Action plan*

1 Look at the exam instructions and sentences A–H.

   1 What is the topic of the five recordings?

   2 What information do you need to listen for?

> **Tip!** Remember that three of sentences A–H aren't needed.

> **Tip!** Don't worry about understanding every word in each recording. It isn't necessary.

2 🎧 ¹ 16 Follow the exam instructions, using the advice to help you. **[You will need to play this recording twice.]**

You will hear five short extracts in which people talk about deciding to take up new interests.

For questions **19–23**, choose from the list (**A–H**) the reason each speaker gives for deciding to take up their new interest. Use the letters only once. There are three extra letters which you do not need to use.

A to help other people

B to make some money

C to pass the time

D to meet new people

E to try to win a prize

F to overcome a fear

G to get fit

H to make a change from their work

Speaker 1	19
Speaker 2	20
Speaker 3	21
Speaker 4	22
Speaker 5	23

> **Tip!** When you check your answers on the second listening, remember that one mistake may have led to others.

Advice

A Three people offer a service, but which one doesn't charge?

B Which speaker had problems with money?

C Be careful – one speaker gives this as a reason for not being interested in the activity.

D Two speakers mention meeting new people, but only one had this as their main aim.

E Two speakers talk about winning competitions, but was that a main reason?

F Think of other expressions for 'overcome' and 'fear'.

G Three speakers talk about being or getting fit, but was that their main purpose?

H Make sure it's the speaker's reason for taking it up, not other people's.

Page 57 *Task information*

 Page 58 *Action plan*

1   Look at the exam instructions.
  1   What kind of recording (e.g. *speech*) is it?
  2   What's the topic?
  3   Who will you hear?

Tip! Don't choose an answer just because you hear the same word or phrase. Listen for the same *idea*.

Tip! For each question, wait until the speaker finishes talking about it before you decide on your answer.

2   🎧 17) Follow the exam instructions, using the advice to help you. **[You will need to play this recording twice.]**

Part 4

You will hear an interview with a woman called Adriana Moretti, who works as a wildlife photographer. For questions **24–30**, choose the best answer (**A**, **B** or **C**).

24   Why did Adriana want to become a wildlife photographer?
  A   She enjoyed travelling to remote locations.
  B   She was very good at taking photos.
  C   She was interested in animal behaviour.

25   Why, according to Adriana, is it easier nowadays to learn how to photograph animals?
  A   The necessary equipment is cheaper than it used to be.
  B   It is possible to learn wildlife photography online.
  C   Cheap international travel means more species can be photographed.

26   Why did Adriana feel uncomfortable while she was trying to take photos of birds?
  A   She was not able to sit down.
  B   Her feet were getting wet.
  C   She was being bitten by insects.

27   How did Adriana feel when she was trying to photograph the crocodile?
  A   afraid that it might try to attack her
  B   worried she may not get the photo she wanted
  C   increasingly bored with waiting to take the picture

28   Adriana has still never taken photos of
  A   a tiger in India.
  B   a snow leopard in China.
  C   a polar bear in Russia.

29   What disadvantage does Adriana say her work has?
  A   She sometimes feels lonely when she is working abroad.
  B   She doesn't see her family as often as she would like to.
  C   She always has to go where the agency tells her.

30   Adriana believes it is becoming harder to get work as a wildlife photographer because
  A   so many photos of wildlife are available on the Internet.
  B   there is a lot of competition for jobs in wildlife photography.
  C   people are becoming less interested in wildlife.

Tip! If you're not sure, mark the two most likely. Choose from those on the second listening.

Advice

24 *Think of other ways of saying 'interested in animal behaviour'.*

25 *Think of expressions that mean 'photographic equipment' and 'cheaper'.*

26 *Which two of A–C does she say were not a problem?*

27 *What is the focus of the question? Which of the adjectives in A–C describes this?*

28 *Which two of these animals had she already photographed?*

29 *Choose the one that is a problem for Adriana, not for other people.*

30 *Which of A–C does Adriana say isn't true and which doesn't matter?*

Page 59   *Task information*

Revising expressions

1 **For questions 1–6, decide which is the best thing to do in Speaking Part 1: A, B or C.**

1 When you go into the room for the Speaking test, you should

A always use formal language and call the examiners 'Sir' or 'Madam'.

B be polite and friendly to the examiners and your partner.

C ignore everyone until the exam questions begin.

2 When the examiner asks you a question, you should

A just say 'yes', 'no' or 'maybe'.

B answer with a speech you prepared earlier.

C give full answers, with reasons and examples.

3 In Part 1 you should always reply to

A the examiner who asks you the questions.

B the other candidate.

C the examiner who does not ask the questions.

4 While the other candidate is speaking, you should

A listen to what he or she says.

B think about something else.

C correct any mistakes he or she makes.

5 If you don't understand a question, you should

A say nothing.

B pretend you understand and talk about something else.

C politely ask the examiner to repeat it.

6 During the test, you

A can use words in your first language if you need to.

B must talk only in English.

C may ask the examiner to translate certain words.

2 **If possible, work in pairs. Think of three expressions for:**

1 asking for repetition   *Sorry, I didn't catch that.*

2 adding information

3 giving a reason

4 giving an example.

Test 2 Exam practice Speaking Part 1

 Page 60 *Action plan*

If you have a partner, answer these questions in pairs.

Tip! Don't spend *too* long thinking before you reply to the examiner's questions.

Part 1   2 minutes (3 minutes for groups of three)

Interlocutor First, we'd like to know something about you.
- What do you like about living in your home town?
- What kind of music do you enjoy listening to? Why?
- Which musical instrument would you like to play really well? Why?
- What is your earliest memory of your school days?
- Which school subject do/did you most enjoy? Why?

Tip! Think of a different way of saying something if you don't know a particular word.

Tip! Don't worry about getting every factual detail correct (e.g. the exact year you started school). It's a language test, not a job interview!

Page 61   *Task information*

Revising expressions

1 **Are statements 1–10 about Speaking Part 2 true (T) or false (F)?**
Correct the false statements.

  1 Each candidate has to discuss two photos.
  2 Each candidate has to speak for two minutes.
  3 When you see the photos, you should plan what you're going to say.
  4 You need to compare the photos and also answer the question about them.
  5 You must describe everything you can see in both pictures.
  6 You can correct yourself if you make a mistake when you're speaking.
  7 You should check your watch to see when you have to stop.
  8 You should listen to your partner without interrupting them.
  9 You need to be ready to answer a question about your partner's photos.
  10 At the end of your partner's turn, you can comment on what he/she has said.

2 **If possible, work in pairs. Think of three expressions to:**
  1 say which picture you're talking about
    The picture on the left shows …
  2 compare the pictures
  3 contrast the pictures
  4 say what you think is possible in the pictures
  5 say which of two things you'd prefer to do.

Page 63 *Action plan*

1 Look at the exam instructions below and photos A, B, C and D on pages C6–C7.

   1 What does each of A–D show?

   2 What does Candidate A have to do?

   3 What does Candidate B have to do?

2 If you have a partner, do this exam task in pairs.

Tip! Remember that the examiner will give you spoken instructions for the task, but you can also read them at the top of the page.

Tip! As soon as you see the pictures, start thinking about what you will say, making a mental note of any useful vocabulary you can use. If you're not sure what's in the pictures, don't worry. You can use expressions like *it seems that ..., it might be ...* or *perhaps ....*

Tip! Don't be so worried about making mistakes that you say very little. The examiners can't give you good marks if you don't speak enough.

Part 2

Interlocutor	*(Candidate A)*, it's your turn first. Here are your photographs on page C6. They show **people writing in different situations**.
	I'd like you to compare the photographs, and say **why you think the people are writing.**
	(Candidate B), **Do you prefer to write to people by hand or by using a keyboard?**
	Now, *(Candidate B)*, here are your photographs on page C7. **They show snow falling in different places.** I'd like you to compare the photographs, and say **how the snow might affect the different people.**
	(Candidate A), **How would you feel if you were in a car in that weather?**

Tip! When you practise for Part 2, if possible get a friend to time you as you speak. Try to keep speaking for the full minute!

Page 64   *Task information*

Revising expressions

1   Fill in the gaps in this text about Speaking Part 3, using the words in the box. There is one word that you do not need.

all	each	two	agreement
reasons	decision	polite	suggestions
turns	diagram		

In Part 3 the examiner gives you a **(1)** .... and explains what you have to do. Then you discuss **(2)** .... idea or possibility shown, taking **(3)** .... with your partner so that you both speak for about the same amount of time. At this stage you make **(4)** .... , for instance by saying *how about …?*, and give your own opinions, where possible giving **(5)** .... to support them. You can disagree with your partner, but if you do, it's important to be **(6)** .... After about **(7)** .... minutes, when you have talked about **(8)** .... the things shown, the examiner will ask you to make a **(9)** .... about which of them to choose, but it doesn't matter if you can't reach an **(10)** .... with each other. The important thing is to keep talking for another minute.

2   If possible, work in pairs. Think of three expressions to:
   1   make a suggestion
   2   ask if someone agrees with your suggestion
   3   agree with somebody's suggestion
   4   disagree politely with somebody's suggestion
   5   give reasons for disagreeing with somebody's suggestion.

Page 65 *Action plan*

1 Study the exam instructions and the diagram on page C8.

    1 What kind of things does the diagram show?

    2 What two things do you have to do?

2 If you have a partner, do this exam task in pairs.

Tip! Take turns with your partner to start talking about each thing. Don't worry if the other candidate seems to know more English than you. Make sure you speak for about the same length of time as him/her.

Tip! You can check with the examiner – or your partner – if you're not sure what you have to do. Don't try to talk about something different from the topic in the instructions.

Tip! There's no right or wrong decision, and it doesn't matter if you can't agree on a decision.

Part 3

Interlocutor Now, I'd like you to talk about something together for about two minutes. *(3 minutes for groups of three)*

I'd like you to imagine that a group of young people are going to spend a weekend walking in the mountains. Here are some of the items they are thinking of taking with them and a question for you to discuss.

First you have some time to look at the task.

Now, talk to each other about why they should take these items.

Thank you. Now you have a minute to decide which is the most important of these items to take.

Page 66 *Task information*

Revising expressions; predicting discussion points

1 Choose the correct alternative in *italics* in these sentences about Speaking Part 4.

1 The topic of Part 4 *links and extends / is different from* the topic of Part 3.

2 If the examiner asks you a question that you don't understand, you can *see it written down / ask him or her to repeat it*.

3 If you don't know any facts about the topic, *say what you think about it / say nothing at all*.

4 During Part 4 you speak to *the other candidate all the time / the person who speaks to you*.

5 You *are allowed to / are not allowed to* disagree with what your partner says.

6 You should encourage your partner to say *more / less* about the topic.

7 You should *take no notice of / listen carefully to* your partner while he or she is speaking.

8 At the end of the test, you should *shake hands with / say 'goodbye' and 'thank you' to* the examiners.

2 If possible, work in pairs. Think of three expressions to:

1 ask for someone's opinion

2 give your opinion

3 try to change someone's opinion.

3 Think about the topic of Part 3 (walking in the countryside). What issues do you think the examiner might ask you to discuss?

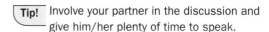 **Tip!** Involve your partner in the discussion and give him/her plenty of time to speak.

Test 2 Exam practice   Speaking   Part 4

 Page 67   *Action plan*

Work in a group of three if possible. Decide who will be the 'examiner' and who
will be the 'candidates'. Answer these questions as fully as you can.

Part 4   4 minutes (6 minutes for groups of three)

Interlocutor Select any of the following questions, as appropriate.

- What do young people gain from the experience of going on adventure holidays?

- Why do some people enjoy going camping in the countryside?

- Do you think that visitors to the countryside damage the environment? Why?/Why not?

- At what age should young people be allowed to go on holiday without their parents? Why do you think so?

- What are the biggest dangers if you are walking in the mountains?

- Should people who take unnecessary risks in the countryside have to pay if they need to be rescued? Why?/Why not?

Select any of the following prompts, as appropriate.

- **What do you think?**
- **Do you agree?**
- **And you?**

Thank you. That is the end of the test.

Tip! Remember that there are no correct or incorrect answers or opinions. The important thing is to say what you think!

For questions **1–8**, read the text below and decide which answer (**A**, **B**, **C** or **D**) best fits each gap. There is an example at the beginning (**0**).

Mark your answers **on the separate answer sheet**.

Example:

0   **A** branch   **B** item   **C** piece   **D** part

0	A	B	C	D
	⎵	⎵	⎵	▬

Checking your mobile phone

How often do you check your phone? For many of us, our phone is an essential **(0)** .... of everyday life, but apparently we are spending an increasing amount of time checking it for information without being **(1)** .... of doing so.

Research in Helsinki shows that phone checking **(2)** .... lasts less than 30 seconds on each occasion, and usually **(3)** .... of opening a single application such as social media. The study also found many users check their mobiles throughout the **(4)** .... day, and that what they check is often **(5)** .... with particular contexts. For instance, when travelling to work or college, people tend to check their email; if they are bored, they get a quick **(6)** .... on the latest news.

Checking this frequently can easily become a habit, which some say can **(7)** .... us from more important things. Others, though, believe that being able to **(8)** .... so much new information so quickly makes life far more interesting.

1 **A** sensitive   **B** cautious   **C** sensible   **D** conscious

2 **A** virtually   **B** typically   **C** widely   **D** suitably

3 **A** consists   **B** composes   **C** involves   **D** includes

4 **A** complete   **B** total   **C** normal   **D** entire

5 **A** attached   **B** assumed   **C** associated   **D** accompanied

6 **A** update   **B** revision   **C** review   **D** upgrade

7 **A** disturb   **B** distract   **C** disrupt   **D** distribute

8 **A** capture   **B** import   **C** obtain   **D** seize

For questions **9–16**, read the text below and think of the word which best fits each gap. Use only **one** word in each gap. There is an example at the beginning (**0**).

Example: | 0 | T | H | E | | | | | | | | | | | | | | | |

The Australian city of Perth

Perth, (0) .... capital of the state of Western Australia, has been described as one of the most remote cities (9) .... Earth. Founded in 1829 and named after Perth in Scotland, it grew rapidly in the late nineteenth century (10) .... a result of the discovery of gold in the state. Nowadays it has a population of around two million people, and many of (11) .... were born outside Australia. This has led (12) .... Perth becoming a culturally diverse city, in (13) .... of the fact that the nearest large town is over 2,000 kilometres away, with well-established communities from southern Europe and South-East Asia (14) .... particular. The city's five universities have also attracted students from (15) .... over the world. Young people find much to enjoy in and around Perth on (16) .... of its outdoor lifestyle, which offers a wide range of activities including swimming at its many beaches, cycling both in town and countryside, and visiting nearby nature reserves.

For questions **17–24**, read the text below. Use the word given in capitals at the end of some of the lines to form a word that fits in the gap **in the same line**. There is an example at the beginning (**0**).

Write your answers **IN CAPITAL LETTERS** on the separate answer sheet.

Example: | 0 | G | R | O | W | T | H | | | | | | | | | | | | |

Advertising in schools

In certain countries, there has been rapid **(0)** .... in the spending power   **GROW**

of teenagers. Realising this, firms are aiming even more of their **(17)** ....   **PRODUCE**

at young people, and **(18)** .... they are doing this by advertising directly   **INCREASE**

in schools. These companies see children as the **(19)** .... of the future,   **CONSUME**

and hope that when they become adults they will maintain their **(20)** ....   **LOYAL**

to brands they first started buying in their youth.

As a result, many **(21)** .... are keen to supply equipment to schools,   **MANUFACTURE**

sponsor sports activities or provide students with kit that carries their logo.

Other firms install machines selling snacks and drinks, and these are often highly

(22) .... for both the companies and the schools.   **PROFIT**

There is, however, considerable **(23)** .... about whether this is a good   **AGREE**

idea. Some claim these firms provide a useful service, but others argue that

these machines encourage **(24)** .... eating habits at a time when many   **HEALTH**

doctors are concerned about the diet of the young.

For questions **25–30**, complete the second sentence so that it has a similar meaning to the first sentence, using the word given. **Do not change the word given.** You must use between **two** and **five** words, including the word given. Here is an example (**0**).

Example:

0   Nobody had ever done my hair like that before.

HAD

I'd .... like that before.

The gap can be filled by the words 'never had my hair done' so you write:

Example: | **0** | NEVER HAD MY HAIR DONE |

Write only the missing words **IN CAPITAL LETTERS** on the separate answer sheet.

---

25   The storm left very few trees standing.

WERE

Hardly .... after the storm.

26   'What's the height of that building?' I asked the guide.

HOW

I asked the guide .... was.

27   The new printer is very similar to the old model.

MUCH

There is not .... the new printer and the old model.

28   Simon wouldn't apologise for being so rude.

WAS

Simon refused to .... for being so rude.

29   What attracts people so much to this city is its nightlife.

FIND

What people .... this city is its nightlife.

30   It's unlikely our firm will manage to win the contract.

SUCCEED

Our firm is unlikely .... the contract.

You are going to read an extract from a novel. For questions **31–36**, choose the answer (**A**, **B**, **C** or **D**) which you think fits best according to the text.

Alex North felt uncomfortable. With little time to pack, she'd forgotten her professional suit jacket. So she was wearing flat black boots, dark denim jeans, a long-sleeve white T-shirt and fawn shawl; she looked more like a protestor than a journalist. Tiredness added to her misery. As she made her way home last night, she had expected to be enjoying a Saturday morning lie-in. But after a panicky 2 a.m. phone call from her editor Gerome, a tense cab ride to the hospital and then an 8 a.m. plane from Heathrow to Prague, her day was far off course. She'd had little rest on the plane; after embarrassing herself by flinging out an arm in her sleep and hitting the crew-cut young American sitting next to her, she sat awake and rigid for the rest of the flight.

Bernie was meant to be in Prague covering this story.

line 16 'It all boils down to this, my dear,' he had said last night during their evening out with the others from the office. 'If I can get a really good story at the international conference, I might actually retire. Job done. Go home. It's that important.'

Bernie left earlier than Alex, keen to go over his notes and finish packing. Alex stayed out with the rest of her colleagues, and she'd barely made it into bed when Gerome had called to pass on the terrible news. Bernie was in hospital. His wife said he collapsed when he got home. The doctors diagnosed a stroke. Alex was so horrified that the Prague conference, and the large number of protestors expected to turn up there, was the last thing on her mind. But Gerome insisted she go in Bernie's place. He told her to get a good night's sleep, knowing full well she would get dressed and rush to visit Bernie.

Bernie Cook and his wife Laura had been like parents to Alex since she arrived in London from Australia four years ago. 'Aren't you a bit old to be a trainee?' was the first of many questions Bernie asked. Alex explained that journalism wasn't her first career choice. She tried her hand at accounting, but found her office job was torture. Her three-year communications degree was far more satisfying, but left her jobless and penniless at age 28. So off to London it was, with a traineeship at the UK's best investigative daily newspaper, living in the city's smallest, cheapest flat and sustained by a weekly roast dinner at Bernie and Laura's.

Anyone overhearing Alex and Bernie talking would never think there was a 30-year age difference. Bernie's passion for political debate – and conspiracy theories – kept Alex enthralled for hours. And his talent for journalism had rubbed off. Seeing him lying there unconscious, so still and frail, was a shock to Alex. Laura looked visibly withered, leaning over Bernie's face as if frightened she might miss something if she glanced away. She barely looked up long enough to give Bernie's iPad to Alex so she could study his notes for the assignment.

Alex pretended to feel confident as she hurried across Charles Bridge towards the conference venue – Prague Castle. She was staying near the Old Town Square, in the predictably modest hotel booked by Bernie. Alex had politely endured the hotelier's gossip; Bernie always said the people were the best thing about Prague. But Alex loved the pastel feel of the city, the swans on the river and the winding cobbled streets. She knew her way around, having visited once before with a forgettable ex-boyfriend. She recalled being more impressed with Prague than with him. It was no wonder the relationship petered out like all the others.

31 In the first paragraph, what do we learn about Alex?

    A She was excited at the prospect of working in Prague.

    B She was feeling better after sleeping on the plane.

    C She was worried her clothes were unsuitable for work.

    D She had known it was going to be a busy night.

32 What does 'it all boils down to this' on line 16 mean?

    A as far as I am aware

    B this is the only problem

    C what annoys me is this

    D to sum up the situation

33 When Alex's boss rang her

    A he expected her to do everything he said.

    B he told her to go to the airport immediately.

    C he said she had to cover the story in Prague.

    D he wanted her to go to Bernie and Laura's house.

34 Why did Alex become a journalist?

    A She was an unemployed graduate looking for work.

    B She was attracted by the high salaries in London.

    C Bernie had encouraged her to do the same job as him.

    D That was what she had always wanted to be.

35 What upset Alex at the hospital?

    A Laura's attitude towards her.

    B Bernie's notes about the conference.

    C What Bernie said when she arrived there.

    D The contrast with how Bernie usually was.

36 How did Alex feel when she arrived in Prague?

    A She was sad her ex-boyfriend wasn't there with her.

    B She was glad to be there again.

    C She was sure she would do a good job there.

    D She liked the luxury accommodation she had there.

You are going to read a magazine article about outdoor ice skating. Six sentences have been removed from the article. Choose from the sentences **A–G** the one which fits each gap (**37–42**). There is one extra sentence which you do not need to use.

Go skating in Sweden this winter

Forget crowded indoor ice rinks. Once you've skated on natural ice, there's no going back.

It was the question on all of our minds, but I asked it: 'How do you know when the ice isn't safe to skate on?' Niklas, our calm Swedish guide, rubbed his chin, thought for a moment, then offered up the wisdom of a lifetime spent playing around on frozen water. 'When it breaks,' he said with a broad smile.

The comment wasn't exactly reassuring, but his easy confidence was. As long as it was just jokes being cracked, maybe we'd be all right after all. Niklas, a maths teacher when having breaks from pursuing his favourite hobby, was not entirely joking about his attitude to ice. **37** [   ] The fact that strong ice makes a deeper sound under one's feet than thin ice does is a useful clue.

Our group of beginners was feeling rather nervous as we stood at the edge of a vast frozen bay that first day. Niklas tried his best to persuade us to move forward but, like hesitating penguins on an iceberg, no-one wanted to take the first step. **38** [   ] 'Look at your faces,' shouted Niklas to the happily smiling group, racing along behind him.

Our expressions had been far less joyful the previous evening on being told that a five-hour drive would follow our flights into Sweden's Arlanda airport. That hadn't been the plan; but then, in the world of natural ice skating, no-one expects very much from plans. With its 100,000 lakes and continuous sub-zero winter temperatures, Sweden has no shortage of ice. **39** [   ] For instance, too much overlying snow and you get a bumpy, uncomfortable ride; a sudden thaw and vast areas become unusable.

Perfect conditions must be sought out, and don't last. **40** [   ] Niklas had received a message via social media about Stigfjorden, a shallow, island-studded bay around 50 kilometres north of Gothenburg on the west coast.

There we quickly discovered skating in the open air is a wonderfully leisurely activity. Push off with one skate and you can go 10 metres with ease. Two or three quick kicks at the surface and you accelerate like a top-class sprinter. **41** [   ] We weren't yet ready to skate that kind of distance, but we certainly had a wonderful sense of freedom.

Our best day was at Vattern, one of Europe's biggest lakes and also one of its clearest. In ideal conditions, this clarity creates a phenomenon known as 'glass ice'. The rocky lake bottom stretched beneath us, three metres below a surface so perfect it was unseen. My tentative first steps left scratches; it felt like vandalising a classical sculpture. As my confidence grew, so did my speed. The sensation as I raced across the invisible ice was astonishing, somewhere between floating, falling and flying. Then there was a sharp noise from all around us. **42** [   ] No one had to say it. We were skating on very thin ice.

A That was the reason for our unscheduled journey from one side of the country to the other.

B Ten minutes later we laughed at our earlier caution as we slid across the smooth surface, our joy as limitless as our surroundings.

C The skates consisted of removable blades that fastened to the toes of our specialist boots like cross-country skis.

D At first I ignored it, but when thin cracks began to appear I thought it wise to return to solid ground.

E After our first session on the ice had ended, we were not surprised to be told that covering 250 kilometres in a single day is quite possible.

F The Swedes adopt a common-sense approach: they are cautious, they test as they go, and they use ears – as well as eyes – to check it.

G This is not always suited to skating, however.

You are going to read an article about the effects of tourism on local people. For questions **43–52**, choose from the people (**A–E**). The people may be chosen more than once.

Which person

misses a place they used to go to as a child?	**43**
states that tourism provides a considerable number of jobs for local people?	**44**
wishes local people had opposed the construction of certain holiday homes?	**45**
claims that tourism has destroyed a traditional industry?	**46**
blames the tourist industry for spoiling the local countryside?	**47**
feels that the presence of people from other cultures benefits the local community?	**48**
criticises the behaviour of tourists in their town?	**49**
says the town is wealthier than it was before it became a tourist resort?	**50**
believes that most of the profits from the local tourist industry go abroad?	**51**
is not convinced that so-called green tourism actually benefits the environment?	**52**

Living with tourism

Five people describe how tourism has affected their home town.

A   Leonor Sousa

It can't be denied that tourism has attracted investment, which has certainly raised living standards here, but the cost in other respects has been extremely high. Take the effect on the environment, for instance. When my parents were young this used to be an area of fields and woods, but now everything is covered in concrete. The tourists themselves aren't responsible for this; it's the construction companies, property developers and estate agents who are to blame because they're the ones making all the money. They're all based in the big cities and bring in their own people, so they hardly create any employment at all for local residents.

B   Yusuf Demir

When I was growing up in my home town there was a path I used to walk along to go to school, and last summer I went to see if it was still there. It was, but the view from it had changed completely. Now there is a vast shopping mall, with a cinema and cafés alongside. I don't actually mind that, because it means there are lots more things to do, and I also like the fact that it has a really international atmosphere. It's good for local people to meet visitors from other parts of the world, try new kinds of food and hear about different ways of living.

C   Matt Walker

Tourism has changed this town so much, even in the years since I was at junior school. In those days there was a football pitch near the harbour where we would kick a ball around, but it's gone now, which is a pity. In the harbour itself luxury yachts owned by people from richer parts of the country have replaced the fishing boats, to the extent that there is now no sign of what used to be the main source of income and employment locally. In the evenings the town is certainly a lot livelier, but sometimes people start doing things they would never think of doing back in their own home towns, and then the police have to be called.

D   Trisha Chandra

I was just a child when tourism first took off here and those incredibly ugly houses were built for summer visitors. The residents really should have protested about that. It was all the fault of the town council, who only ever thought in the short term and seemed to give planning permission to anyone who applied to build anything. Nowadays there's talk of ecological tourism, but that's just a way of making people feel less guilty about the harm they are doing by making a few insignificant changes, such as re-using towels in their hotel rooms.

E   Daniela Navarro

I know some of the new hotels and holiday apartment blocks are unattractive, and that the bars, restaurants and nightclubs that cater for tourists have changed the nature of the town, but without them unemployment – particularly among the young – would be far worse than it currently is. That, though, is as far as the economic benefits to the town go, as the only ones making any real money out of all this are the big tour operators and the owners of hotel chains, none of whom are actually based in this country. Also, very few tourists learn our language. I know it must be difficult for them because most of them are quite old, but it means there's little communication between us and them.

You **must** answer this question. Write your answer in **140–190** words in an appropriate style.

---

1   In your English class you have been talking about sending rockets into outer space and the enormous cost of the space programme. Now your English teacher has asked you to write an essay.

Write an essay using all the notes and give reasons for your point of view.

Should we spend money on exploring space?

Notes

Write about:

1   spending priorities

2   what we might discover in space

3   .... (your own idea)

Write an answer to one of the questions **2–4** in this part. Write your answer in **140–190** words in an appropriate style.

---

2   A group of English-speaking students would like to go walking in your country. The group leader has asked you to write a report that includes the following information:

   • the best place in the countryside to go walking

   • the best time of year to walk there

   • what the group should take with them when they go there.

   Write your **report**.

3   You see this announcement in a lifestyle magazine.

Reviews of electronic devices wanted Which electronic device have you used recently? Write a review of it describing the device, explaining how to use it and saying whether it is good value for money.

   Write your **review**.

4   You have received this email from your English-speaking friend Alex.

   From: Alex

   Subject: your visit

   I'm really pleased to hear that you can spend a week with me and my family here. People say this is one of the world's most exciting cities!

   What kind of places would you like to visit and what would you like to do downtown?

   We can either use public transport or hire bikes to get around. Which would you prefer?

   See you soon,

   Alex

   Write your **email**.

01 You will hear people talking in eight different situations. For questions **1–8**, choose the best answer, **A**, **B** or **C**.

1   You hear a film review on the radio.
    What criticism does the reviewer make?
    A   the acting is poor
    B   the music is unsuitable
    C   the story is difficult to follow

2   You hear two students talking about a holiday abroad.
    What do they agree about?
    A   Foreign travel is harmful to the environment.
    B   It is becoming more expensive to travel abroad.
    C   Holidays are more enjoyable if you go abroad.

3   You hear a woman talking on the radio about a place called Dolphin Bay.
    Where did she first hear about Dolphin Bay?
    A   on the Internet
    B   on the radio
    C   on television

4   You overhear a woman talking outside the post office.
    Why had she gone to the post office?
    A   to collect a parcel
    B   to buy stamps
    C   to send a parcel

5   You hear part of a discussion on local radio.
    What is the programme about?
    A   building new housing
    B   protecting wildlife
    C   improving road safety

6   You hear a man talking about motorcycling.
    What does he regret?
    A   riding his motorcycle too fast
    B   doing a particular journey by motorcycle
    C   buying a motorcycle

7   You overhear a student talking about her new college.
    How does she feel about the college?
    A   She is finding some of the lessons difficult.
    B   Some of her new classmates are unfriendly.
    C   It is too far away from her home.

8   You overhear a driving instructor talking to a learner after the lesson has ended.
    What mistake did the learner make?
    A   He ignored a road sign.
    B   He was driving too fast.
    C   He failed to look in the mirror.

02) You will hear a student called Fiona Doyle talking about living in the countryside after growing up in a city. For questions **9–18**, complete the sentences with a word or short phrase. **[You will need to play this recording twice.]**

Moving to the countryside

Fiona says the lack of **(9)** .... in the countryside created a contrast at night.

Some rooms in the house can be rather **(10)** .... in winter.

At first, the **(11)** .... made it difficult for Fiona to sleep in the house.

Fiona finds she tends to **(12)** .... later in the day than when she was in the city.

In the countryside, Fiona sees **(13)** .... from her bedroom window.

Fiona sometimes finds the slowness of the **(14)** .... where she lives rather irritating.

Out in the countryside, Fiona sometimes can't get **(15)** .... from friends.

The nearest **(16)** .... is almost two kilometres away from where Fiona lives.

Fiona says you need to have a **(17)** .... in the country, but not in the city.

Fiona won't have to travel as far to the **(18)** .... as she would from her old home.

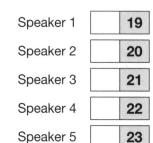 You will hear five short extracts in which people are talking about difficult situations they have been in. For questions **19–23**, choose from the list (**A–H**) what each speaker says they did in each situation. Use the letters only once. There are three extra letters which you do not need to use. **[You will need to play this recording twice.]**

A   I contacted the emergency services.

B   I found it impossible to remain calm.

C   I did what I had been trained to do.

D   I followed someone else's advice.

E   I made a decision I later regretted.

F   I helped people reach safety.

G   I was tempted to ignore what had happened.

H   I had an argument with someone.

Speaker 1 [   ] **19**

Speaker 2 [   ] **20**

Speaker 3 [   ] **21**

Speaker 4 [   ] **22**

Speaker 5 [   ] **23**

2 04 You will hear an interview with travel writer Amy McCarthy about her first experience of travelling abroad. For questions **24–30**, choose the best answer (**A**, **B** or **C**). **[You will need to play this recording twice.]**

24 Why did Amy want to go abroad?

   A She wanted to find a job in another country.

   B Her friends had invited her to go with them.

   C She felt she was good at learning languages.

25 Amy and her friends decided to go to Ibiza because

   A it was cheaper than similar destinations.

   B there were lots of things to do there.

   C none of them had been there before.

26 When she was at the airport, Amy felt

   A glad she had taken sandwiches with her.

   B worried that she might miss her plane.

   C annoyed that she had spent so much.

27 Amy's friend Carla annoyed Amy because Carla

   A sometimes left dirty dishes in the living room.

   B often forgot her keys when she went out.

   C wouldn't do any food shopping.

28 Why didn't Amy phone her family?

   A She didn't have enough credit left on her phone.

   B She forgot that she had promised to call them.

   C She didn't want them to hear her sounding unhappy.

29 What did Amy regret doing?

   A booking three weeks at the apartment

   B taking the wrong items on holiday with her

   C agreeing to take it in turns to cook meals

30 What were Amy's feelings when she got home?

   A She never wanted to go on holiday with friends again.

   B The holiday had been a useful learning experience.

   C Next summer she would look for work abroad.

Part 1   2 minutes (3 minutes for groups of three)

Interlocutor First of all, we'd like to know something about you.

- When do you spend time with your family? What do you do together?
- How well do you know your neighbours?
- Do you often go on social media sites? Why?/Why not?
- Do you ever buy things online? Why?/Why not?
- Tell us about an interesting journey you have been on.

Part 2   4 minutes (6 minutes for groups of three)

Interlocutor In this part of the test, I'm going to give each of you two photographs. I'd like you to talk about your photographs on your own for about a minute, and also to answer a question about your partner's photographs.

(Candidate A), it's your turn first. Here are your photographs on page C9. They show **people celebrating special occasions.**

I'd like you to compare the photographs, and say **what you think the people are enjoying about the occasions.**

All right?

Candidate A ....

Interlocutor Thank you.

(Candidate B), **What kind of special occasion do you enjoy most?**

Candidate B ....

Interlocutor Thank you.

Now, (Candidate B), here are your photographs on page C10. They show **people queuing in different places.**

I'd like you to compare the photographs, and say **how you think the people in each queue are feeling.**

All right?

Candidate B ....

Interlocutor Thank you.

(Candidate A), **When do you find yourself waiting in queues?**

Candidate A ....

Interlocutor Thank you.

| Part 3 | 4 minutes (3 minutes for groups of three) |

Interlocutor Now, I'd like you to talk about something together for about two minutes. (3 minutes for groups of three)

I'd like you to imagine that you need to buy some new clothes, but without spending too much money. Here are some of the ways you could buy them and a question for you to discuss.

First you have some time to look at the task.

Show candidates the diagram on page C11. Allow 15 seconds.

Now, talk to each other about **the advantages and disadvantages of each way of shopping for clothes.**

Allow two minutes (three minutes for groups of three).

Interlocutor Thank you. Now you have a minute to decide **which way would save you most money.**

Allow one minute for pairs or groups of three.

Thank you.

| Part 4 | 4 minutes (6 minutes for groups of three) |

Interlocutor Select any of the following questions, as appropriate.

- When is the best time to go shopping?
- Is it better to go shopping alone or with friends? Why?
- Do you think online shopping will eventually replace going to the shops? Why?/Why not?
- Which items do you think are best to buy second-hand? Why?
- Some people say we too often buy things we don't really need. What do you think?
- Do you think people should borrow money to buy things they want?

Select any of the following prompts, as appropriate.

- **What do you think?**
- **Do you agree?**
- **And you?**

Thank you. That is the end of the test.

For questions **1–8**, read the text below and decide which answer (**A, B, C** or **D**) best fits each gap. There is an example at the beginning (**0**).

Mark your answers **on the separate answer sheet**.

Example:

0   **A** job   **B** place   **C** role   **D** part

| 0 | A ▯ | B ▯ | C ▬ | D ▯ |

Pets can improve your life

The **(0)** .... of animals in helping people recover from a range of health and emotional problems has long been **(1)** .... recognised. Now a survey reported in the *Journal of Personality and Social Psychology* appears to show that owning a pet can **(2)** .... healthy individuals, too. A number of experiments, **(3)** .... by two universities in the United States, indicate that pet owners are generally happier, healthier, fitter, more confident and better able to **(4)** .... with everyday issues than non-owners.

The researchers discovered that individuals have just as **(5)** .... a relationship with the key people in their lives, in **(6)** .... words family and friends, as they have with their pets. And although they found no **(7)** .... that people choose emotional relationships with pets over relationships with other people, a study of university students showed that owning a pet helped them **(8)** .... over the break-up of a relationship with a partner.

1 **A** mainly   **B** deeply   **C** highly   **D** widely

2 **A** benefit   **B** improve   **C** profit   **D** contribute

3 **A** carried   **B** conducted   **C** governed   **D** operated

4 **A** cope   **B** handle   **C** treat   **D** survive

5 **A** near   **B** close   **C** true   **D** actual

6 **A** additional   **B** other   **C** different   **D** alternative

7 **A** signal   **B** support   **C** evidence   **D** example

8 **A** get   **B** pull   **C** take   **D** go

For questions **9–16**, read the text below and think of the word which best fits each gap. Use only **one** word in each gap. There is an example at the beginning (**0**).

Example: | **0** | T | O | | | | | | | | | | | | | | | | | |

Eating at university

According **(0)** .... a recent study, 59 per cent of university students miss lunch each week, and 65 per cent can't **(9)** .... bothered having breakfast. Eating regular meals, it seems, is very **(10)** .... one of the average student's top priorities, yet the same study shows that well **(11)** .... half of those questioned wish they'd learnt how to cook at school.

Having a good diet can make settling into life at university much easier. That's **(12)** .... it makes such good sense to learn how to prepare a few meals, even **(13)** .... they are only basic things like soup or egg on toast.

If there's a shared kitchen, it's a good idea to take turns cooking for everyone, **(14)** .... than making meals one after the other, **(15)** .... can lead to tensions when people are feeling hungry. Sharing the cooking means there's a variety of meals, nobody has to cook every day, and **(16)** .... is more, it saves money.

For questions **17–24**, read the text below. Use the word given in capitals at the end of some of the lines to form a word that fits in the gap **in the same line**. There is an example at the beginning (**0**).

Write your answers **IN CAPITAL LETTERS** on the separate answer sheet.

Example: | 0 | A | P | P | E | A | R | A | N | C | E | | | | | | | | |

Preparing for an interview

Before you go to an interview, think about your **(0)** .... When you make   **APPEAR**

your **(17)** .... of clothes, avoid anything too casual but don't go to the   **CHOOSE**

other extreme of wearing items that are so formal you feel **(18)** .... in   **COMFORT**

them.

Make sure you know the exact **(19)** .... of the building where the interview   **LOCATE**

will take place. There's nothing worse than **(20)** .... trying to find the right   **DESPAIR**

place as the time for it to begin rapidly approaches.

Once you reach the firm's offices, remember that the interview starts there. You

never know who you might meet in lifts, corridors or waiting rooms, so try to make

a good **(21)** .... on everyone.   **IMPRESS**

When you go into the interview room, show you have **(22)** .... in yourself,   **CONFIDENT**

and strike an appropriate balance between formality and **(23)** .... Bear   **FRIEND**

in mind that people tend to make a **(24)** .... about someone they have   **JUDGE**

met within a few minutes.

For questions **25–30**, complete the second sentence so that it has a similar meaning to the first sentence, using the word given. **Do not change the word given.** You must use between **two** and **five** words, including the word given. Here is an example (**0**).

Example:

0   I think it would be a good idea to call a meeting.

   FAVOUR

   I .... a meeting.

The gap can be filled by the words 'am in favour of calling' so you write:

Example:	**0**	AM IN FAVOUR OF CALLING

Write only the missing words **IN CAPITAL LETTERS** on the separate answer sheet.

---

25   We haven't seen each other for two years.

   BEEN

   It's .... we last saw each other.

26   'You didn't tell me the truth, Emilio' said Carmen.

   ACCUSED

   Carmen .... her the truth.

27   I really think you ought to arrive on time for the meeting.

   LATE

   I strongly advise .... for the meeting.

28   Even though we played badly we won the match.

   SPITE

   We won the match .... badly.

29   The flying time to Singapore is six hours.

   FLY

   It .... to Singapore.

30   I didn't realise that the beach was so far from the campsite.

   SUCH

   I didn't realise that ....long way from the beach to the campsite.

You are going to read an article about the actor Daniel Radcliffe, who played the role of Harry Potter in the films. For questions **31–36**, choose the answer (**A**, **B**, **C** or **D**) which you think fits best according to the text.

Daniel Radcliffe

I first meet Daniel Radcliffe at the offices of his agent, just before he takes to the stage for an evening performance of *The Cripple Of Inishmaan*. He's wearing tight jeans, no glasses, and is a super ball of energy. He is extraordinarily polite, slim, well turned out. If you'd never seen him before, you might assume he was a children's television presenter. But at the age of just 24 he has 16 movies behind him, eight of them Harry Potter blockbusters. It feels as if he's been with us forever. The funny thing is, apart from the facial hair, he doesn't really look any different from the schoolboy wizard who made his screen debut in 2001.

Yet over the past half-dozen years, it seems he has done everything he could to distinguish himself from Harry in the parts he has chosen to play. Radcliffe disagrees with this, saying 'I pick films based on scripts and directors and parts. I'm not interested in making films I've seen before. There's nothing more exciting to me when I read a script than originality. That's all it's governed by, there's no master plan to distance myself from Potter.'

He says he doesn't want to sound ungrateful. 'I know that Potter is going to be with me for the rest of my life, so to try to stop people talking about that any more is stupid. It's just a fact of your life, so you can't get annoyed by it. You have to accept the fact that you were involved in this incredibly cool thing and though you might not always be happy with the work you did on it, the opportunity it has given you to make a career for yourself is amazing.'

Was he aware how much Harry would change his life when he was offered the part? 'No, I knew I was signing on for the first two, that four books had come out. Warner, the film company, genuinely didn't know at that stage if they were going to make more than one film. If it flopped, then they certainly weren't going to put up all that money again.' Did he ever consider exercising his opt-out clause? 'By the third film, I thought, if there's a time to get out, it's now; there's still enough time for another actor to come in and establish himself. For a while, I thought, if I do all of them, will I be able to move on to other stuff or should I start doing other stuff now? But in the end I decided I was having way too much fun. And actually there aren't many great parts out there for teenage boys, certainly not as good as Harry Potter.'

Nowadays, of course, he is incredibly wealthy. I ask whether he sometimes worries people might socialise with him purely because of that. He laughs, and says people are going to be sadly disappointed if they befriend him for his lavish spending. 'Anyone who is my friend knows that I don't spend money. So they can hang around with me as much as they like and they still aren't going to get anything. Haha!' But, he says, he has never had a problem with working out who to trust. 'I'm a fairly good judge of character, and I have a small but very close circle of friends. I'm not looking to recruit new friends, though I'm actually very open with people. I had a similar conversation with myself when I was about 17, the first time somebody had really betrayed that trust, and I said to myself you have two options: you either become totally insular and shut down and not let anybody into your life ever, or you can continue to be open and amiable when you meet people, and trusting, and occasionally get hurt. And I do think that is the best way.'

31 What do we learn about Daniel in the first paragraph?

    A He is now working in TV programmes for children.

    B His appearance has changed considerably since his childhood.

    C He is currently acting in the theatre.

    D He is amused by the way he looked in his early films.

32 What does Daniel say about his current work?

    A He likes to make changes to the film scripts he is given.

    B He sometimes has to accept roles he would rather reject.

    C He finds it difficult to play roles that are not Harry.

    D He denies he chooses roles as unlike Harry as possible.

33 What does Daniel appear to be criticising in the third paragraph?

    A Some of his acting in the Harry Potter films.

    B The overall quality of the Harry Potter films.

    C The effect of playing Harry Potter on his career.

    D Attempts to talk to him about Harry Potter.

34 When Daniel was first asked to play Harry Potter

    A he thought the first film would be made on a low budget.

    B he thought that only two Harry Potter books would be published.

    C he had no idea how many films in the series there would be.

    D he only wanted to be in the first film in the series.

35 Why did Daniel eventually decide to be in every film?

    A He thought nobody else could play the role of Harry.

    B He was enjoying making the films so much.

    C He never considered doing any other kind of work.

    D He knew it would eventually lead to different roles.

36 How does Daniel feel about friendship?

    A He believes he knows how to choose friends well.

    B He would like to have more friends than he has now.

    C He finds it difficult to trust people these days.

    D He likes to be generous to those he is close to.

You are going to read an article about the effects of electronic devices on human interaction. Six sentences have been removed from the article. Choose from the sentences **A–G** the one which fits each gap (**37–42**). There is one extra sentence which you do not need to use.

Have we lost the ability to focus on a single task?

Daniel Goleman thinks so. Here, the bestselling science writer argues that we have become a species distracted by modern technology.

The little girl's head only came up to her mother's waist as she hugged her mum, and held on fiercely as they rode a ferry to a holiday island. The mother, though, didn't respond to her, or even seem to notice: she was absorbed in her tablet computer all the while.

Something similar happened a few minutes later, as I was getting into a shared taxi van with nine students who that night were journeying to a weekend getaway. Within a minute of taking their seats in the dark van, dim lights came on as every one of them checked a phone or tablet. **37 [   ]** But mostly there was silence.

The indifference of that mother, and the silence among the students, are symptoms of how technology captures our attention and disrupts our connections. Teenagers, the future of humanity, are at the centre. In the early years of this decade their text message monthly count rose to 3,417, double the number just a few years earlier. **38 [   ]** The average American teen now gets and sends more than a hundred texts a day, about 10 every waking hour. I've seen a kid texting while he rode his bike.

Digital interaction comes at a cost in face time with real people, through which we learn to understand non-verbal communication such as body language. The new generation of natives in this digital world may be skilful on the keyboard, but they can be hopeless when it comes to reading behaviour face-to-face, in real time. **39 [   ]** Today's children are growing up in a new reality, one where they are connecting more with machines and less with people than has ever been true in human history.

Then there are the costs of attention decline among adults. In Mexico, an advertising representative for a large radio network complains, 'A few years ago you could make a five-minute video for your presentation at an advertising agency. Today you have to keep it to a minute and a half. **40 [   ]** ' Faced with problems like this, some workplaces have banned laptops, mobile phones, and other digital tools during meetings.

A college professor who teaches film tells me he's reading a biography of one of his heroes, the legendary French director François Truffaut. But, he finds, 'I can't read more than two pages at a time. **41 [   ]** I think I'm losing my ability to maintain concentration on anything serious.'

After not checking her mobile for a while, a publishing executive confesses she gets 'a nervous feeling. You miss that moment of excitement you get when there's a text. You know it's not right to check your phone when you're with someone, but it's an addiction.' So she and her husband have an agreement: 'When we get home from work we put our phones in a drawer. **42 [   ]** But now we try to get closer to each other instead. We talk.'

A This is why they are unaware they upset others by stopping to read a text in the middle of a conversation.

B If you don't, everyone starts checking for messages.

C After that the temptation to go online and see if I have any new email becomes impossible to resist.

D A few words were occasionally muttered while they texted or looked through social media pages.

E If it's in front of me I get anxious; I've just got to check it.

F In extreme cases, some sleep all day and play these games all night, rarely stopping even to eat.

G Meanwhile, studies show, the average time they spent talking on the phone dropped significantly.

You are going to read an article in which six students talk about their university. For questions **43–52**, choose from the students (**A–F**). The students may be chosen more than once.

Mark your answers **on the separate answer sheet.**

Which student

is studying at a university that was not their first choice?	43
has found it easier to make friends at university than they had expected?	44
wishes they had more time to take part in social activities?	45
chose their university partly because a relative had recommended it?	46
complains about the travelling time from their accommodation to the city centre?	47
wants to continue studying at the same university after they graduate?	48
praises the approach to teaching at their present university?	49
decided to study at the university because of its location?	50
sought the opinions of current students before choosing a university?	51
is finding student life less expensive than they had expected?	52

My university

Six first-year students say what life is like at their universities.

A Zehra Erdogan

There's a club here for just about every sport or social activity you can think of, and they're a great way to get to know other students. I'd wondered whether I might feel lonely here with my family so far away, but I needn't have worried. There's a group of us who get on really well, and two are already talking about doing research here once they've finished their first degrees. That's my aim too.

B Ben Robertson

I had to take out a loan to cover my costs as a student here, but I quickly found there were all kinds of expenses I hadn't thought of, such as the cost of getting into town and back from the student village, where I live. The buses aren't cheap and it takes ages to get there, too, but I didn't check that when I chose this university. That's something I could have done quite easily online, but unfortunately I didn't. Actually, the main reason I came here was to be with my friends, who applied at the same time as I did.

C Anika Mishra

I found it relatively easy to settle in here, just as I thought I would, really. I'd done some research on the various places offering the course I wanted to do, and what I found particularly helpful were the online comments by people actually studying in each one. Actually, this one had always appealed to me as my aunt did a research degree here and said it was a good place to live and study, though unlike her I think I'll move onto another university once I've graduated.

D Lotte Peeters

Before I came here, people had been telling me I'd find it hard to live on my government grant, but that hasn't really been the case because during my free time I'm nearly always in the halls of residence with the other students. There's so much to do there that it doesn't matter that they're quite a long way from the university, which is right in the centre of town. In fact, I can't do half the things I'd like to do because I'm a medical student and I'm just too busy studying to join any more societies or clubs.

E Pablo Flores

Universities in different parts of the world tend to be quite similar in some ways, such as the international mix of students, the atmosphere and even the buildings, but something I like about studying here is that you spend a lot of your time in seminars with a tutor. So, nearly a year on, I'm actually quite relieved I had my application rejected by the top university on my list: if I'd gone there I would have spent all day taking notes in lectures. The only downside is that the cost of living is quite a bit higher in this country.

F Maxim Kuznetsov

As I have family and friends living in several nearby countries, I needed to be somewhere close to an airport offering budget flights. So studying here looked ideal, and though I've noticed prices are quite high in the city, there's plenty to do on campus and I rarely need to go there. Actually, the only time I do that is when some of my old friends come to visit me, and on those occasions we take the train. There's a good service into town, and I can get a discount by using my student card.

You **must** answer this question. Write your answer in **140–190** words in an appropriate style.

1 You have had a discussion in your English class about the importance of studying particular subjects at secondary school. Now your English teacher has asked you to write an essay.

Write an essay using all the notes and give reasons for your point of view.

All students should study science subjects in every school year.

Notes

Write about:

1 interesting lessons

2 future careers in science

3 .... (your own idea)

Write an answer to **one** of the questions **2–4** in this part. Write your answer in **140–190** words in an appropriate style.

2   You see this announcement in an English-language magazine.

> ### The best advice I have ever had
>
> What is the best piece of advice you have ever been given?
>
> Who gave you that advice? Why was it so helpful to you?
>
> Write an article answering these questions. We will publish the best articles in our next edition.

Write your **article**.

3   You see this advertisement in your local English-language newspaper.

> ### Shop assistants wanted for summer work
>
> We require shop assistants to work with English-speaking customers in our department stores this summer. Positions are available in the following departments:
>
> - fashion
> - music
> - electronic equipment
>
> Write to Emma Murphy at Holiday Stores saying which department interests you and why, and explain why you would be suitable for the job.

Write your **letter**.

4   A number of English-speaking students are planning to stay with host families in your country this summer. Their teacher has asked you to write a report on what times people usually have their meals there, what differences there are in the kinds of food that young people and older people prefer, and which dishes you would particularly recommend.

Write your **report**.

05 You will hear people talking in eight different situations. For questions **1–8**, choose the best answer, **A**, **B** or **C**.

1   You hear a man and a woman talking about a department store.
     What is the woman's opinion of the store?
     A   The prices are generally reasonable.
     B   There is a wide range of items on sale.
     C   Most of the assistants are very helpful.

2   You hear a woman asking a man questions in a city-centre street.
     She wants him to
     A   take part in a survey.
     B   give her directions to a bus stop.
     C   use public transport more often.

3   You hear part of a radio interview with a newspaper's science reporter.
     He thinks that it is
     A   less of a problem than some scientists say.
     B   not taken seriously enough by governments.
     C   now too late to stop it happening.

4   You hear a recorded message when you phone a hotel.
     What should you do if you want to stay there an extra night?
     A   press one
     B   press two
     C   press three

5   You hear two parents talking after watching their son play in a football match.
     What do they agree about?
     A   Their son was the best player in his team.
     B   The referee was unfair to their son's team.
     C   Their son's team should have won the game.

6   You hear a man talking on the radio about a castle by the sea.
     How does the speaker suggest visitors get to the castle?
     A   by car
     B   on foot
     C   by public transport

7   You hear a woman talking about her computer.
     Why couldn't she email her friend?
     A   Her computer wasn't online.
     B   A virus had damaged her computer.
     C   She couldn't remember her password.

8   You overhear a man leaving a message on an answering machine.
     Why is he phoning?
     A   to apologise for something he has done
     B   to ask the other person for some advice
     C   to thank the person for something they did

2 06 You will hear a man called André Laroque talking about a luxury railway journey in Canada. For questions **9–18**, complete the sentences with a word or short phrase. **[You will need to play this recording twice.]**

A four-night trip on the Canadian Pacific Railway

André says that the route his train took is **(9)** .... kilometres long.

André says that Calgary was placed first in a list of the world's **(10)** .... cities.

André was particularly impressed by how **(11)** .... the mountains along the route are.

André says that pictures of trains on **(12)** .... have made the Canadian Pacific internationally famous.

André was pleased to find that he had his own **(13)** .... in his compartment on the train.

André was surprised that there was only one **(14)** .... for the sixteen passengers.

During dinner on the train, André listened to live **(15)** .... music.

André was disappointed not to see a **(16)** .... when the train stopped so passengers could go on a walk.

As they went down a hill called Big Hill, André saw a lot of **(17)** .... coming from the train.

Towards the end of his journey, André saw the biggest **(18)** .... of its kind in North America.

2 07) You will hear five short extracts in which people talk about why they changed their job. For questions **19–23**, choose from the list (**A–H**) the main reason each person gives for their last change of job. Use the letters only once. There are three extra letters which you do not need to use. **[You will need to play this recording twice.]**

A   to work outdoors

B   to have more responsibilities

C   to work fewer hours each week

D   to have longer holidays

E   to earn more money

F   to move to a new location

G   to improve career prospects

H   to have a new challenge

Speaker 1		19
Speaker 2		20
Speaker 3		21
Speaker 4		22
Speaker 5		23

2 08 You will hear a radio interview with Lily Jenkins, whose favourite sport is windsurfing. For questions **24–30**, choose the best answer, **A**, **B** or **C**. [**You will need to play this recording twice.**]

24 How did Lily feel when she first tried windsurfing?

  A worried that her feet would slip off the board

  B glad that she had watched a training film first

  C impatient to start moving quickly over the water

25 According to Lily, how long does it usually take to learn to windsurf?

  A It depends on the equipment you use.

  B It takes less time than you expect.

  C It varies from person to person.

26 Lily believes she quickly learnt the basics of windsurfing because

  A she had lessons at a windsurfing school.

  B her friend was an excellent teacher.

  C she was already an experienced surfer.

27 What safety advice does Lily give beginners?

  A Try to make sure your sail never falls into the water.

  B Tell someone on land how you can be identified at sea.

  C Practise windsurfing on lakes rather than at sea.

28 Lily now thinks that as a complete beginner she should have

  A used a bigger sail.

  B rented a board and sail.

  C bought a smaller board.

29 Nowadays, what does Lily most enjoy about windsurfing?

  A learning new techniques

  B developing her muscles

  C forgetting everyday worries

30 Lily thinks that eventually she will

  A become a windsurfing instructor.

  B take part in windsurfing competitions.

  C have to give up windsurfing.

Part 1   2 minutes (3 minutes for groups of three)

Interlocutor First of all, we'd like to know something about you.

- Do you prefer to spend your free time indoors or outdoors? Why?
- Tell us about a website you like to visit.
- What kind of films do you like to watch? Why?
- Who is your favourite film or TV actor? Why?
- Tell us about a time you went shopping.

Part 2   4 minutes (6 minutes for groups of three)

Interlocutor In this part of the test, I'm going to give each of you two photographs. I'd like you to talk about your photographs on your own for about a minute, and also to answer a question about your partner's photographs.

(Candidate A), it's your turn first. Here are your photographs on page C12. **They show people taking photographs in different situations.**

I'd like you to compare the photographs, and say how you think the people being photographed probably feel.

All right?

Candidate A ....

Interlocutor Thank you.

(Candidate B), **Do you like having your photograph taken?**

Candidate B ....

Interlocutor Thank you.

Now, *(Candidate B)*, here are your photographs on page C13. They show **parks in different city centres**.

I'd like you to compare the photographs, and say **what the different people are enjoying about being in these parks.**

All right?

Candidate B ....

Interlocutor Thank you.

(Candidate A), **Which park would you prefer to be in?**

Candidate A ....

Interlocutor Thank you.

Part 3   4 minutes (5 minutes for groups of three).

Interlocutor Now, I'd like you to talk about something together for about two minutes. (3 minutes for groups of three)

I'd like you to imagine that a discussion is taking place about modern lifestyles.

Here are things that some people say would be difficult to live without and a question for you to discuss.

First you have some time to look at the task.

Show candidates the diagram on page C14. Allow 15 seconds.

Now, talk to each other about **why some people think these things would be difficult to live without.**

Allow two minutes (three minutes for groups of three).

Interlocutor: Thank you. Now you have a minute to decide **which thing most people would find most difficult to live without.**

Allow one minute for pairs or groups of three.

Thank you.

Part 4   4 minutes (6 minutes for groups of three)

Interlocutor Select any of the following questions, as appropriate.

- What do you think is the most useful device that has been invented in the last 20 years? Why?
- Do you think modern technology reduces or increases stress? Why?
- Which jobs do you think might be replaced by robots in the future?
- How have advances in technology changed the way people communicate with each other?
- Some people say that certain computer games are too violent. What do you think?
- What changes would you like to see science or technology make to the world?

Select any of the following prompts, as appropriate.

> - **What do you think?**
> - **Do you agree?**
> - **And you?**

Thank you. That is the end of the test.

For questions **1–8**, read the text below and decide which answer (**A**, **B**, **C** or **D**) best fits each gap. There is an example at the beginning (**0**).

Mark your answers **on the separate answer sheet**.

Example:

0   **A** beneath   **B** lower   **C** minus   **D** less

0	A	B	C	D
	☐	☐	▬	☐

Mars on Earth

The centre of Antarctica, where winter temperatures frequently fall to **(0)** .... 80 degrees centigrade and for four months each year there is **(1)** .... darkness 24 hours a day, is one of the most extreme environments on Earth. It is also by **(2)** .... the most similar place to the surface of Mars, which is why a **(3)** .... of thirteen scientists from the European Space Agency have spent nine months at a base there.

They have been studying the physical and psychological **(4)** .... on humans of living in extreme conditions, in order to obtain a better understanding of the difficulties humans will **(5)** .... during the long flight to Mars and their stay there. Of course, space is **(6)** .... Antarctica in that astronauts have to adapt to weightlessness, but the base is 3,200 metres above sea **(7)** .... making it difficult to breathe there – as it can be on space flights. They have also, like space travellers, experienced strong feelings of being **(8)** .... off from civilisation.

1   **A** regular   **B** constant   **C** repeated   **D** maintained

2   **A** far   **B** much   **C** large   **D** long

3   **A** crew   **B** cast   **C** gang   **D** team

4   **A** results   **B** effects   **C** issues   **D** risks

5   **A** oppose   **B** dare   **C** challenge   **D** face

6   **A** unlike   **B** contrary   **C** unfamiliar   **D** different

7   **A** height   **B** level   **C** depth   **D** scale

8   **A** broken   **B** cut   **C** kept   **D** taken

For questions **9–16**, read the text below and think of the word which best fits each gap. Use only one word in each gap. There is an example at the beginning (**0**).

Example: | 0 | | S | I | N | C | E | | | | | | | | | | | | | | | |

Marathon in the mountains

The Ultra-Trail of Mont Blanc is an extreme marathon held annually **(0)** .... 2003 in the mountains of France, Italy and Switzerland. Widely regarded **(9)** .... one of the toughest races in the world, the Ultra-Trail takes place in August, **(10)** .... temperatures frequently range from over 30°C at the lowest points of the course, to well **(11)** .... freezing at the highest.

An Olympic marathon is 42.5 kilometres long, but **(12)** .... one is over 160 kilometres in length and includes nine mountain peaks. That involves climbing a total of approximately 9,500 metres, **(13)** .... is considerably higher than Everest. In **(14)** .... of, or perhaps because of this, the annual event has become increasingly popular with runners, to **(15)** .... an extent that the numbers have had to be limited to 2300. Only about half of these, **(16)** .... average, are likely to finish the course, in times that typically vary from 20 hours to over 45.

For questions **17–24**, read the text below. Use the word given in capitals at the end of some of the lines to form a word that fits in the gap **in the same line**. There is an example at the beginning (**0**).

Write your answers **IN CAPITAL LETTERS** on the separate answer sheet.

Example: | 0 | R | E | A | S | O | N | A | B | L | E | | | | | | | |

Jobs in the future

In twenty years' time, which jobs will people still be doing, and which is it
(**0**) .... to assume will have gone forever? Today's young people should   **REASON**
give that question careful (**17**) .... before choosing a career. Clearly   **CONSIDER**
there will continue to be a need for staff in (**18**) .... professions such as   **EXIST**
medicine that involve caring for others, and also for people able to persuade, like
(**19**) .... and lawyers.   **POLITICS**

There will of course be no (**20**) .... of jobs in science and technology,   **SHORT**
particularly for individuals able to (**21**) .... in newer fields such as   **SPECIAL**
biotechnology and microbiology.

On the other hand, the already rapid (**22**) .... of jobs to robots will   **LOSE**
speed up even further, as they replace workers not only in manufacturing but
also in the (**23**) .... industry. And as robots learn how to stack shelves,   **CONSTRUCT**
take over at check-outs or send us our online shopping, it won't be long before
most supermarket jobs have (**24**) .... , too.   **APPEAR**

For questions **25–30**, complete the second sentence so that it has a similar meaning to the first sentence, using the word given. **Do not change the word given.** You must use between **two** and **five** words, including the word given. Here is an example (**0**).

Example:

0   My little brother went to see the big match by himself.

OWN

My little brother went .... to see the big match.

The gap can be filled by the words 'on his own' so you write:

Example:	0	ON HIS OWN

Write only the missing words **IN CAPITAL LETTERS** on the separate answer sheet.

---

25   Amanda woke up late because she'd forgotten to set her alarm.

HAVE

If Amanda hadn't forgotten to set her alarm she .... late.

26   This Internet browser works far better than the others.

NEARLY

The other Internet browsers don't .... this one.

27   'Can I borrow your phone for a minute, Jack?' asked Emma.

WHETHER

Emma asked Jack .... phone.

28   Raymond has so much skill as an artist that his drawings look like photographs.

SUCH

Raymond is .... artist that his drawings look like photographs.

29   I wish I hadn't stayed up so late last night.

BED

I should .... last night.

30   Our departure was delayed because another flight arrived late.

CAUSED

The delay to our departure .... arrival of another flight.

You are going to read an extract from a novel. For questions **31–36**, choose the answer (**A**, **B**, **C** or **D**) which you think fits best according to the text.

Night flight

The flight is busy and the last few passengers to board are searching for places to stow their hand luggage. The Asian woman in the seat next to me is in her late twenties, probably travelling on business. I am wondering if I should talk to her when the man in the window seat shows up and we have to let him in. She settles back in the middle seat. When I try to strap myself back in I find she's picked up the buckle of my belt by accident and we look at each other and laugh.

'What have you been doing in Bangalore?' I ask.

'My office is there. It's where I'm based.' I notice that she has a North American accent. She tells me she works for a multinational company that makes clothing and that she is on her way to Thailand. She has to visit a couple of factories and meet with some other people from the company. She's also trying to complete her PhD thesis, which is on a laptop she has under the seat in front of her. While she's talking she puts her passport away in her bag and I see she's Canadian.

She asks me what I do and I tell her. Then I ask her some more about her job and she tells me about that. By this time we are in the air and climbing towards our cruising altitude. The cabin is quiet, lights still dimmed, just the gentle sound of the air conditioning and the murmur of conversations. The flight to Singapore is three and a half hours. I can't decide whether to attempt sleep. It is nearly midnight and it hardly seems worth it. The man in the window seat has put on eye-shades and has an inflated pillow around his neck. He has slipped down in the seat with his head lolling to one side, his blanket pulled up to his chest. The woman shows no inclination to sleep so I ask her where she grew up.

She tells me her father is a medical doctor and that he went to Canada before she was born. They spent a few years in Montreal but most of the time she lived in Saskatchewan. 'It was OK,' she says. 'There are things happening there, it's not as dull as you might think.' She tells me sometimes in the winter it would get down to minus sixty.

'Really it was minus thirty,' she says. 'But the wind chill factor made it feel like minus sixty. I remember them saying on the weather forecast "human flesh will freeze in 1.4 seconds." Things like that.'

'I've never been anywhere that cold,' I say.

'Somehow it didn't feel that bad,' she says. 'It was like a dry cold. When the sun was shining it didn't seem that cold. It makes your skin kind of tingle. We used to play out in it. You can get seriously cold and not realise it. When you're back indoors your face and hands ache as the blood comes back. I suppose that is how polar   *line 52* explorers end up losing toes. They don't realise how cold they are.'

'I suppose so,' I say. There's a pause in the conversation and I wonder what to say next.

'I guess you get the other extreme living in India.'

'Bangalore is fine,' she says, 'though we need rain. The drought is very bad in south India right now.'

The woman asks me how I got into my present job and I tell her a bit about my life. At least I tell her the story which over time has fashioned itself into what I call my life. It's not that I'm being deliberately secretive or deceitful. I just don't know how to talk about what really happened.

31 What do we find out about the woman in the first paragraph?

   A She is annoyed at having to change seats with another passenger.

   B She finds a mistake she makes amusing.

   C She wants to get on with her work during the flight.

   D She has difficulty finding room for items she brought on board.

32 What does the woman say at the beginning of the conversation?

   A She has Canadian nationality.

   B She usually works in Thailand.

   C She is currently both studying and working.

   D She is going to work for a different employer.

33 Why does the writer stay awake throughout the flight?

   A There is a lot of mechanical noise on the plane.

   B Nobody else on board seems to want to sleep.

   C Some of the passengers are talking loudly.

   D He would not be able to sleep very long.

34 The woman talks about temperatures in Canada to show that

   A it could sometimes be extremely cold in Montreal.

   B India is a more pleasant country to live in than Canada.

   C the place where she grew up could be interesting.

   D in Saskatchewan children had to stay at home all winter.

35 What does 'that' refer to in line 52?

   A failing to notice how cold some parts of the body really are

   B wearing clothes that do not cover the skin in very cold weather

   C playing games outside in extremely low temperatures

   D going into a warm place straight from somewhere much colder

36 The writer mentions the weather in India because

   A he realises the woman wants to change the subject.

   B he wants to keep the conversation going.

   C he finds the weather an interesting topic to discuss.

   D he had wanted to ask the woman about it while she was talking.

You are going to read an article about returning to work after being away on holiday. Six sentences have been removed from the article. Choose from the sentences **A–G** the one which fits each gap (**37–42**). There is one extra sentence which you do not need to use.

Just because I've been on holiday doesn't mean I have to be happy

'Holiday hangover', 'back-to-work blues', 'post-travel depression' – it's a well-known condition, and I'm suffering from it.

My cat. My tortoise. My friends. My bed. The list reads the same every time, but I still write it. I write it on the last day of every holiday, to convince myself that going home isn't so bad. Then I feel utterly miserable. There are plenty of things I'm not great at – driving, maths, returning library books on time – but the thing I'm worst at is coming back to work after a holiday.

It's an extreme case of being selfishly miserable. To have had a lovely sunshine break and then return to the office, where everyone has been working hard without restaurant lunches or morning swims, with a face like thunder is terribly bad manners. **37** ☐ Given the number of names for it – 'holiday hangover', 'back-to-work blues', 'post-travel depression' – it's a well-known condition.

In a recent survey conducted by a travel website, 82 per cent of the 1,254 people asked experienced post-holiday misery. **38** ☐ Probably just before they logged on to a job vacancy website or started fantasising about retraining for work in the countryside.

Even if you manage to avoid end-of-holiday panic, and you feel refreshed, relaxed and ready to face the world of work, you're guaranteed to walk into stress, conflict and injustice. **39** ☐ Or the surprise departmental reorganisation that took place while you were away.

Still, it could be worse. Over three-quarters of people questioned said that their holiday depression lasted for a month. **40** ☐ Perhaps they should have saved their cash and not bothered going.

After years of practice, I've come up with a few things that help. A bit. The first is the list mentioned above. **41** ☐ Unlike some people I know, I can't just roll off an intercontinental flight and roll in to the office. The third is concentrating on getting through the first day back at work without running away, making a grand plan for a new life or spending (too much) time on my own tearfully looking at my holiday photos saying to myself: 'I can't believe this is my life.'

I feel sorry for my poor colleagues having to look at my long face today, but at least by having my break now I'm getting my bad mood in early. **42** ☐ Then I can support them in their hour (month?) of need. I might even lend them one of my pets.

A By September, on the other hand, when the schools go back and the main summer-holiday season is over, I'll be back to normal.

B The most content, with both their home and working life, appear to be those who stay at home all summer.

C For instance, that highly important task you left with a colleague that's been ignored and later caused your email inbox to turn toxic.

D At least, though, I'm not the only fed-up wage slave to feel like this.

E The next one is making sure I have a day off everything between getting home and going to work.

F Also, over two-thirds of them answered the next question, 'Are you usually glad to be home after a holiday abroad?' with a – presumably unhappy-sounding – 'No'.

G Longer by at least a fortnight, I'd guess, than the holiday they'd taken.

You are going to read a newspaper article about an Olympic athlete. For questions **43–52**, choose from the paragraphs (**A–D**). The paragraphs may be chosen more than once.

Which paragraph

gives an example of Jessica having good luck? | 43 |

refers to the role of Jessica's family in helping her achieve success? | 44 |

suggests it is surprising that Jessica does not understand herself better? | 45 |

mentions a previous sporting disappointment that Jessica had? | 46 |

explains why Jessica is so popular with the local public? | 47 |

explains why another athlete was surprised at Jessica's performance? | 48 |

mentions a painful childhood memory? | 49 |

suggests that Jessica's appearance can give a misleading impression? | 50 |

says that Jessica's relationship with someone can sometimes be difficult? | 51 |

contrasts Jessica's personality on and off the track? | 52 |

 **Jessica Ennis: heptathlon Olympic champion**

A There have been many great Olympic athletes in recent years, but few have been taken to their country's heart quite as warmly as gold medal winner Jessica Ennis. Her quiet determination to succeed, her good humour when faced by setbacks and the absolute joy she showed when finally becoming Olympic champion have all contributed to this, as has the difficulty of the sport she has chosen to compete in: the heptathlon. This involves turning in world-class performances in seven track and field events over two days. At first sight, Jessica – at just 1.65 metres and 57 kilos – may seem an unlikely winner of such a physically demanding sport, but once the action begins it soon becomes clear she has the speed, strength and endurance to beat anyone.

B Jessica recognises that her normally easygoing nature is transformed into something much fiercer when she has to compete. She knows that success only comes from being highly motivated and totally focused on each event. In her autobiography *Unbelievable*, she talks of the way she was picked on at school by bigger girls because of her background and lack of size, and how that has made her determined to succeed, particularly against taller and stronger athletes. She also points out that she is not from a particularly sporting family and that her sister 'absolutely hates sport', but says she was introduced to athletics by her parents, who have continued to give her encouragement and support throughout her career as an athlete. Her mother was born in the UK and her father in Jamaica.

C She gets on well with her family, as she does with her husband Andy, saying she dislikes conflict and wherever possible avoids arguments with people. The only exception is her trainer Chell, with whom she has a row 'every day'. And although Jessica is a psychology graduate, she is unable to explain how she acquired the tremendous self-discipline that has enabled her to keep training to Olympic gold medal standard while so many others have given up along the way. Of course, at that level nothing can be taken for granted, as she discovered when a sudden injury put her out of the Beijing Games. She describes that as the lowest point in her career. Typically, though, Jessica bounced back, and once fit again began training just as hard as ever.

D By the time of the London Games in 2012 she was in the best shape of her life, and on this occasion she was fortunate enough to remain free of injury. Some of the times she recorded in the heptathlon were so fast that she would have achieved good positions in the finals of track events such as the 200 metres. That brought to mind a race won two years earlier against the world champion, who couldn't believe she had lost to someone who trained for seven different events. Since the London Olympics, Jessica has continued to take part in competitions, receiving numerous awards including World Sportswoman of the Year. She has also featured on a special postage stamp and has had a post box in her home city of Sheffield painted gold in her honour.

You **must** answer this question. Write your answer in **140–190** words in an appropriate style.

1   In your English class you have been discussing holidays in schools and colleges. Now your English teacher has asked you to write an essay.

Write an essay using all the notes and give reasons for your point of view.

Should students have a long summer holiday or should terms be longer?

Notes

Write about:

     1   which is better for learning

     2   leisure activities in the holidays

     3   .... (your own idea)

Write an answer to one of the questions **2–4** in this part. Write your answer in **140–190** words in an appropriate style.

---

2   You see this announcement on an English-language website.

> ### Film reviews wanted
>
> Which film have you seen in which something totally unexpected happened? Write a review of the film, describing what happened and why it was so unexpected. Say whether you think other people would enjoy watching the film, too.
>
> The best reviews will appear on our website next week.

Write your **review**.

3   Your English teacher has asked you to write a report on shopping in your area. You should explain which are the most popular shops or shopping centres in your area, say why you think they are popular, and suggest other kinds of shops that you think should open there.

Write your **report**.

4   You see the following announcement in an international magazine.

> ### Articles wanted for publication
>
> Write about a person who is popular or famous in your country.
>
> We will publish the best articles in next month's magazine.

Write your **article**.

(3)01) You will hear people talking in eight different situations. For questions **1–8**, choose the best answer, **A**, **B** or **C**.

1   You hear a man talking on the radio about a new airport terminal.
     Why does he compare the terminal to a factory?
     A   to criticise the way people are treated there
     B   to emphasise the enormous size of the building
     C   to describe its efficiency in processing passengers

2   You hear a man being interviewed for a job.
     He left his previous job because
     A   he wanted to work in a smaller town.
     B   he did not get on with his boss.
     C   he thought his salary was too low.

3   You hear a woman talking about a city she enjoys visiting.
     What does she like most about the city nowadays?
     A   its food
     B   its people
     C   its architecture

4   You hear a man and a woman talking about a hotel they have recently stayed at.
     They agree that
     A   the location was convenient.
     B   the price of the room was reasonable.
     C   the meals were good.

5   You hear a woman talking about buying a clock on the Internet.
     What does she say about it?
     A   The clock had been damaged when it arrived.
     B   The postage cost more than she had expected.
     C   The item cost her less than what it was worth.

6   You hear a bus driver talking about his job.
     Which aspect of his work does he sometimes really dislike?
     A   driving in city traffic
     B   dealing with passengers
     C   starting work early

7   You hear a man talking on the radio about his early life.
     What does he say about his school days?
     A   He regrets not studying harder.
     B   He remains friends with some classmates.
     C   He disliked some of his teachers.

8   You hear a man telling a woman about an art gallery he has visited.
     The man says the art gallery
     A   was too crowded.
     B   had recently moved.
     C   had too few works on display.

 **02** You will hear a young woman called Amanda Murillo talking to a group of college students about Taekwondo, the Korean martial art. For questions **9–18**, complete the sentences with a word or short phrase. **[You will need to play this recording twice.]**

Taking up Taekwondo

Amanda says she was getting bored with going to **(9)** .... every week.

Amanda's **(10)** .... advised her to take up Taekwondo.

At the Taekwondo club, Amanda was told that size and strength was less important than **(11)** ....

Amanda was helped by the fact that she can keep her **(12)** .... quite well.

Amanda says she was more **(13)** .... than some of the male students.

Amanda explains that the students do some **(14)** .... exercises when they have finished running.

Amanda was surprised to find how high she could **(15)** .... after the initial exercises.

Amanda always wears safety equipment on her **(16)** .... , as well as on her hands.

The only serious injury that Amanda has had was to her **(17)** ....

The next colour belt that Amanda wants to get is **(18)** ....

 You will hear five short extracts in which people criticise the computer they use when travelling. For questions **19–23**, choose from the list (**A–H**) the criticism each speaker makes of their computer. Use the letters only once. There are three extra letters which you do not need to use. **[You will need to play this recording twice.]**

A   The sound quality is poor.

B   The battery runs out too quickly.

C   Some applications run slowly on it.

D   The keyboard is difficult to use.

E   The screen is too small.

F   It looks unattractive.

G   It is difficult to connect it to other devices.

H   It is too heavy to carry easily.

Speaker 1	**19**
Speaker 2	**20**
Speaker 3	**21**
Speaker 4	**22**
Speaker 5	**23**

🎧 3 04 You will hear a student called Ahmet Kaya talking about his vacation job, which involves working at night. For questions **24–30**, choose the best answer (**A, B** or **C**). **[You will need to play this recording twice.]**

---

24 Why did Ahmet decide to get a job working at night?

   A The hours were shorter than for day work.

   B It was the only job he was able to get.

   C The pay was better than for day work.

25 What did Ahmet find hard to get used to at first?

   A Going out to work when others were having fun.

   B Not being able to sleep whenever he wanted to.

   C Going to bed when everyone else was getting up.

26 What effect does Ahmet's job have on his social life?

   A He can't see his girlfriend as often as he would like.

   B It makes no difference to how often he sees his friends.

   C At weekends he stays out all night without feeling sleepy.

27 Ahmet finds his working hours convenient because they enable him to

   A enjoy doing exercise far more.

   B travel on public transport when it is less crowded.

   C make medical appointments in the mornings.

28 Ahmet believes that because he works nights he may be more likely to

   A become bad-tempered.

   B catch an illness.

   C have an accident.

29 Owing to his working hours, Ahmet eats

   A just after he finishes work.

   B once during his shift.

   C whenever he feels hungry.

30 What does Ahmet say about the customers who shop there at night?

   A They know the police are watching them all the time.

   B They are usually in less of a hurry than daytime customers.

   C They buy the same kinds of things as daytime shoppers.

| Part 1 | 2 minutes (3 minutes for groups of three) |

First of all, we'd like to know something about you.

- How often do you read newspapers or magazines? (Which do you like most?)
- Do you enjoy travelling long distances? Why?/Why not?
- Which country would you most like to visit? Why?
- What do you most like doing on the Internet? Why?
- What is your favourite computer game? (How often do you play it?)

| Part 2 | 4 minutes (6 minutes for groups of three) |

Interlocutor In this part of the test, I'm going to give each of you two photographs. I'd like you to talk about your photographs on your own for about a minute, and also to answer a question about your partner's photographs.

(Candidate A), it's your turn first. Here are your photographs on page C15. They show **people singing in different places**.

I'd like you to compare the photographs, and say **why the people are singing in these different places**.

All right?

Candidate A ....

Interlocutor Thank you.

(Candidate B), **Which of these singers would you prefer to listen to?**

Candidate B ....

Interlocutor Thank you.

Now, *(Candidate B),* here are your photographs on page C16. They show **people looking at works of art**.

I'd like you to compare the photographs, and say **what you think the people find interesting about the two different kinds of art**.

All right?

Candidate B ....

Interlocutor Thank you.

(Candidate A), **Which of these kinds of art would you rather look at?**

Candidate A ....

Interlocutor Thank you.

| Part 3 | 4 minutes (5 minutes for groups of five) |

Interlocutor Now, I'd like you to talk about something together for about two minutes. (3 minutes for groups of three)

I'd like you to imagine that a local college is organising courses to encourage people to take up new hobbies. Here are some of the courses they are offering and a question for you to discuss.

First you have some time to look at the task.

Show candidates the diagram on page C17. Allow 15 seconds.

Now, talk to each other about **why people might find each course interesting**.

Allow two minutes (three minutes for groups of three).

Interlocutor: Thank you. Now you have a minute to decide **which course people might find most interesting**.

Allow one minute for pairs or groups of three.

Thank you.

| Part 4 | 4 minutes (6 minutes for groups of three) |

Interlocutor Select any of the following questions, as appropriate.
- Why do you think people have hobbies?
- Which hobby would you like to take up? Why?
- Which are the most popular hobbies in your country? Why do you think that it is the case?
- Why do you think some people like to collect items?
- Some people say that nowadays we don't have enough time for hobbies. What do you think?
- Do you think today's young people have different hobbies from those of older generations? Why?/Why not?

Select any of the following prompts, as appropriate.

- **What do you think?**
- **Do you agree?**
- **And you?**

Thank you. That is the end of the test.

Reading and Use of English   Part 1

For questions **1–8**, read the text below and decide which answer (**A**, **B**, **C** or **D**) best fits each gap. There is an example at the beginning (**0**).

Mark your answers **on the separate answer sheet**.

Example:

0   **A** cause   **B** bring   **C** lead   **D** make

0	A	B	C	D
	⸏	⸏	▬	⸏

Teenagers really do need more sleep

It has long been suspected that lack of sleep can actually **(0)** .... to illness, particularly in young people. Research **(1)** .... students aged 14–19 over a three-week period now appears to **(2)** .... this.

The teenagers wore devices that recorded the movements they made, without being **(3)** .... of them, that indicated they were asleep. The results were then **(4)** .... to the number of illnesses that they had **(5)** .... from during the three weeks, in addition to the number of occasions on which they had been **(6)** .... from school.

What the study showed was that students who slept fewer than seven hours a night caught colds, flu and other relatively **(7)** .... illnesses more often. The problem is that as children enter their teens their natural sleeping patterns change, **(8)** .... in them going to sleep later and therefore wanting to wake up later – but they still have to get up in the morning to go to school.

1   **A** enclosing   **B** combining   **C** associating   **D** involving

2   **A** assure   **B** confirm   **C** defend   **D** justify

3   **A** awake   **B** aware   **C** familiar   **D** sensitive

4   **A** compared   **B** measured   **C** balanced   **D** qualified

5   **A** caught   **B** affected   **C** suffered   **D** experienced

6   **A** outside   **B** remote   **C** distant   **D** absent

7   **A** light   **B** minor   **C** smaller   **D** slight

8   **A** resulting   **B** producing   **C** finishing   **D** forcing

For questions **9–16**, read the text below and think of the word which best fits each gap. Use only one word in each gap. There is an example at the beginning (**0**).

Example: | **0** | | O | U | T | | | | | | | | | | | | | | | |

Music really can reduce that pain

A survey has recently been carried (**0**) .... into the way music affects people in pain, and (**9**) .... it seems to show is that certain songs can actually reduce the sensation of physical pain. About 40% of people suffering (**10**) .... continuous pain said that music helped them feel better, with an even higher figure (**11**) .... young people: a remarkable two-thirds of those taking part (**12**) .... reported to have said it had had a positive effect (**13**) .... their symptoms.

The type of music played appears to make less difference than might (**14**) .... imagined. Pop music, as (**15**) .... as it is fairly gentle and not too loud, is slightly ahead of classical as the favourite for dealing with pain. Researchers believe that listening to your favourite music, (**16**) .... may directly affect both your emotions and your thoughts, can have the very welcome effect of distracting you from what is hurting.

For questions **17–24**, read the text below. Use the word given in capitals at the end of some of the lines to form a word that fits in the gap **in the same line**. There is an example at the beginning (**0**).

Write your answers **IN CAPITAL LETTERS** on the separate answer sheet.

Example: | 0 | | C | O | A | S | T | A | L | | | | | | | | | | | |

Letting the sea in

The small **(0)** .... town of Medmerry has found an unusual way to reduce   **COAST**

the risk of flooding: let the sea in. The scheme involved the **(17)** .... of   **DESTROY**

part of the existing sea wall and the building of seven kilometres of new, higher

(18) .... further inland, closer to local communities. This has led to the   **DEFEND**

(19) .... of a large area of wetland, capable of absorbing the energy of   **CREATE**

the waves and therefore bringing about a **(20)** .... reduction in flooding   **SUBSTANCE**

at times of storm and high tides.

According to environmental scientists, this **(21)** .... project will also turn   **AMBITION**

the whole area into a **(22)** .... nature reserve. It is already attracting large   **MASS**

numbers of birds and other wildlife and eventually it should provide a safe home

for some of the country's most **(23)** .... species. This is bound to attract   **DANGER**

more visitors to the area, although it remains **(24)** .... whether numbers   **CLEAR**

will have to be limited in order to protect the reserve.

For questions **25–30**, complete the second sentence so that it has a similar meaning to the first sentence, using the word given. **Do not change the word given.** You must use between **two** and **five** words, including the word given. Here is an example (**0**).

Example:

0   Awards will be presented at a ceremony next June.

PLACE

An awards ceremony .... next June.

The gap can be filled by the words 'will take place' so you write:

Example: | **0** | WILL TAKE PLACE |

Write only the missing words **IN CAPITAL LETTERS** on the separate answer sheet.

---

25   'Would you like to come to my party, Karen?', the girl said.

INVITED

The girl .... party.

26   Two foolish people took no notice of the warning sign.

PAID

Two foolish people .... the warning sign.

27   The rescue workers had too little food to feed everyone.

NOT

There .... the rescue workers to feed everyone.

28   Jack gets no exercise apart from walking to his car.

ONLY

The .... walking to his car.

29   Sonia wanted to be a nurse so she left her job as a teacher.

GAVE

Sonia .... become a nurse.

30   There's far less noise in this street than there used to be.

NEARLY

In this street, there isn't .... there used to be.

You are going to read an article about doing a degree course from home. For questions **31–36**, choose the answer (**A**, **B**, **C** or **D**) which you think fits best according to the text.

Distance learning

Distance learning can give students the chance to work and learn at the same time.

Nineteen-year-old Jamie Henderson hasn't had what you'd call a typical student experience. Despite wanting to read for a degree in Law, Jamie decided against the usual university route and instead opted to study from home.

'With course fees now so high in this country, I was really put off by all the debt I would have when I came out of university,' he says.

Having made this decision, Jamie was able to look into alternatives – which in the end turned out to be a degree validated by a university through a distance learning provider.

'It was a massive weight off my mind and it was a perfect option for me,' Jamie says. 'It has allowed me to stay near my friends and my family and still work part-time.'

Jamie has been able to take on two part-time jobs – alongside his studies – but has also been free to undertake work experience for a law firm, which has led to a full-time job offer before he has even completed his course.

Jonathan Smith, who is studying for a BA in Business, chose to study via a distance learning course when already in full-time employment.

'I'd studied History, Politics and Economics at school but going to university wasn't even a consideration for me,' he explains. 'My friends were at home, I didn't want to be burdened with debt and I wanted to get straight into a career.'

Jonathan completed a Business and Administration Apprenticeship with the local council. While working as a medical administrator, he studied for a diploma and after 12 months had valuable workplace experience.

'I'd done so well at work that they kept me on. But after six months getting settled into my new role, I was financially stable and ready to progress my career with a degree. I didn't want to give up what I'd achieved to go to university, so distance learning was an appealing choice.'

Obviously, one of the downsides to a distance learning course is that students miss out on the experience of attending university, which means missing out on traditional lectures.

'Reading feedback and instructions from a screen isn't quite the same as talking to someone face-to-face,' Jamie says. 'It's also a lot of work to do on your own. I don't have a close circle of friends going through the same thing, so I can't really ask my peers for help and advice. However, I've found the online *line 46* student forums helpful and the firm I've been working for have offered advice and guidance when I've needed it.'

'I haven't met as many new people as I would have, had I moved away,' says Jamie. 'But I have met new people through work instead. It's just a different type of experience, which is just as rewarding and ultimately, in my opinion, makes me more employable.'

For anyone considering a distance learning course, there are several other factors to be considered; perhaps most importantly, motivation.

'Distance learning isn't an easy option,' says Dr Philip Hallam, Chief Executive Officer of a distance and online learning provider. 'It's going to be a substantial commitment, not only financially but also on your time. We need to make sure that people have really thought it through and understand why they want a degree. You will need to dig deep occasionally.'

Jonathan Smith is confident in the choices he's made regarding education, but believes more could be done to make young people aware of the choices they have.

'When I left school with good qualifications, I was shocked at how little advice was available on options other than university. Everyone is different and education should reflect that. I'm glad I took the route I did and I think it is important that more people have the opportunity to study in a way that suits them.'

31 Why did Jamie decide to do his degree from home?

    A His friends were also studying by distance learning.

    B He had already been offered a full-time job.

    C He wanted to avoid owing a lot of money.

    D He was unable to obtain a place at university.

32 Jonathan's reason for studying from home was that

    A he wanted to remain in his job.

    B the job he was doing was badly paid.

    C his preferred subject wasn't available at university.

    D it was too late for him to apply to university.

33 In line 46, what does 'my peers' mean?

    A the university staff

    B students who have already graduated

    C the management of the firm

    D students of the same age

34 Jamie says that studying from home has enabled him to

    A work with people who were also studying at the same time.

    B improve his chances of finding work in the future.

    C get to know more people than he would have done at university.

    D concentrate on studying rather than spend time socializing.

35 Dr Hallam recommends distance learning for students who

    A dislike having to work very hard.

    B have little time available for study.

    C cannot afford to go to university.

    D know exactly what it involves.

36 In the last paragraph, Jonathan says that young people should

    A be advised not to go to university.

    B be made more aware of the choices they have.

    C apply for work with employers like his.

    D ensure they get high grades at school.

You are going to read an article about dreaming. Six sentences have been removed from the article. Choose from the sentences **A–G** the one which fits each gap (**37–42**). There is one extra sentence which you do not need to use.

Can we control our dreams?

Strange as it seems, the answer is yes – and it could help us solve our problems.

Do we have any influence over the often strange, wandering, night-time journeys in our mind? Could we learn to dream differently, getting rid of repeated nightmares or finding answers to the problems that we cannot solve in daylight hours? Strange though it may seem, the answer is yes. Research suggests that, using practical and psychological techniques, we can influence our dreams and use them to draw on the vast, largely unused resource of our unconscious mind.

Deirdre Barrett, an assistant clinical professor of psychology at Harvard Medical School, is convinced we all have the power to manage our dreams. 'If you want to dream about a particular subject,' she says, 'focus on it once you are in bed. **37** You can also place an object or photo that represents the desired dream on your bedside table,' Barrett says.

Another key factor in using one's dreams creatively is to avoid jumping out of bed the moment you wake up. **38** 'If you don't recall a dream immediately, lie still and see if a thought or image comes to mind,' Barrett says. 'Sometimes a whole dream will come flooding back.'

The point of this second strategy is to make use of the information presented by our unconscious as we sleep. It's hard to put an exact figure on the ratio of our unconscious to conscious mind, but psychologists estimate it to be nine to one. We may believe that thinking is our best problem-solving strategy, but the power of our conscious mind is relatively tiny. **39** So letting the unconscious mind work on it may be healthier and more productive.

Barrett put this to the test in a week-long study with college students; she asked them to use dreaming as a way of finding ways of dealing with a particular problem. **40** 'If we're stuck on a problem, it's our waking, logical way of thinking that's stuck,' Barrett says. 'The dream's power lies in the fact that it's a different manner of thought – it adds to and develops what we've already done while awake.'

Most of us enjoy the rich, pleasantly strange experience of dreaming (and we all dream – some people just don't remember it). But no one enjoys nightmares that keep coming back, or the kind of unpleasant dreams from which you wake sweating. **41** 'It's very common for them to have nightmares about being chased by a monster,' says Delphi Ellis, a counsellor and dream expert. 'This often happens as they get older and become aware of their place in the huge world.'

'As an adult, troubling or frightening dreams are often an indication of difficult issues from the past,' Ellis says. **42** They and all other kinds of dream are an incredibly valuable resource, which most of us simply ignore. So learn to listen to them, even the horrible ones – they're always trying to tell you something.'

A   It's one in which you know you're dreaming as the dream is occurring – the kind of 'dream within a dream' that film characters sometimes have.

B   Even more anxiety-causing, if you're a parent, are the scary ones that have such an effect on your kids.

C   Doing so means you'll lose half of what your dream contained as the day's distractions take over your thoughts.

D   About half of them dreamt about it and one-quarter of them solved it.

E   Since dreaming is so visual, form a picture in your mind of something related to that topic as you fall asleep.

F   The more you ignore dreams like those, the more your unconscious turns up the volume – so a nightmare is that message on full volume.

G   Also, when this consists of going over and over negative or worrying issues in our minds, it is strongly linked with stress, depression and anxiety.

You are going to read a magazine article about bicycles. For questions **43–52**, choose from the people (**A–D**). The people may be chosen more than once.

Which person

bought a second-hand bike?	**43**	
says their new bike is good value for money?	**44**	
found it difficult to slow down at one point?	**45**	
had to take their bike in for repair?	**46**	
needed to put the bike together before they could ride it?	**47**	
bought a new bicycle to replace one that had been stolen?	**48**	
says that riding their bike up hills is tiring?	**49**	
says they wish they had checked the size of the bike sooner?	**50**	
had to get off their bike when they were riding to fix it?	**51**	
compares cycling with another way of keeping fit?	**52**	

A   Jonas Hagen

I bought my new mountain bike online and as soon as it was delivered to my home in kit form I set to work. Once it actually looked like a bike and I'd checked that everything seemed to be working properly, I set off down the road. All went well at first, but later on I had a brief moment of panic when the brakes suddenly failed and I narrowly avoided crashing into a hedge. I adjusted them when I got home, and since then they've been fine. The only other adjustment I've had to make is to raise the seat to the maximum because it turns out this bike is for riders whose inside leg measures considerably less than mine. I should really have noticed that before I bought it.

B   Lili Huang

I originally bought my bike just for occasional use, but now I go everywhere on it. It's great exercise, every bit as good as going to the gym. It feels just the right size for me and somehow I always feel full of energy when I'm on it, even when my friends and I ride into the mountains at weekends. I've only ever had one breakdown, which was when the chain broke. Fortunately there was a garage nearby, where a very kind car mechanic quickly got me back on the road. I don't know what I'd do without my bike, which is slightly worrying because a lot of people round here have had their bikes stolen. That's why I keep it in the hall downstairs, rather than in the street.

C   James Thompson

This is only the second bicycle I've ever bought. It was on offer at the local cycle shop and I think I got something of a bargain because on the whole I've been pleased with it. At first I had some difficulties with the gears, but I managed to sort those out while I was riding. It's a very solid bike, though that does mean it's rather heavy and I wouldn't want to have to push it far if I had a breakdown. It also makes pedalling up steep slopes hard work, although fortunately most of the routes round here are reasonably flat. I don't think it's the kind of bike anyone would want to steal, but I always secure it with a good strong lock just in case. Recently I've also fitted more powerful front and rear lights so that drivers can see me better after dark.

D   Mia Doherty

I actually chose this bike in something of a hurry. I'd left my old one outside the sports centre and when I came back it had just disappeared. I reported it, of course, but that was the last I ever saw of it, and I needed a new one to get to work every day. I probably paid more than I should have done for it, though I know the previous owner had looked after it well and I haven't had any trouble with it. Apart, that is, from a flat tyre which meant I had to stop and mend it on the way home in the pouring rain. Riding it certainly helps keep me fit, and even in weather like that I wouldn't change it for a car. The only incident I've had was when a dog ran out into the road in front of me, but the brakes did their job superbly.

You **must** answer this question. Write your answer in **140–190** words in an appropriate style.

1   You have had a discussion in your English class about teaching materials for schools. Now your English teacher has asked you to write an essay.

Write an essay using all the notes and give reasons for your point of view.

Schools should spend more on computers and software than on textbooks. Do you agree?

Notes

Write about:

   1   which is better for education

   2   which are more enjoyable to use

   3   .... (your own idea)

Write an answer to **one** of the questions **2–4** in this part. Write your answer in **140–190** words in an appropriate style.

---

2   You see this announcement in a travel magazine.

> **Reviews of holiday resorts wanted**
>
> Write a review of a holiday resort you have stayed at. Describe the resort, saying what you enjoyed and did not enjoy about your stay there. Tell us whether you would recommend the resort to other people.
>
> We will publish the most interesting reviews in next month's edition.

Write your **review**.

3   You have seen this announcement on an English-language website.

> **The person from history I most admire**
>
> Who is the person from history that you most admire?
>
> What did they do? What do you particularly admire about them?

Write your **article**.

4   You have received this email from your English-speaking friend Lou.

> **From:** Lou
>
> **Subject:** my visit
>
> I'm really looking forward to my first visit to your area and I'd very much like to find out more about it.
>
> Can you tell me in what ways it has changed in the last 20 or 30 years? What are the most interesting things I could photograph when I'm there?
>
> See you soon.
>
> Lou

Write your **email**.

(3.05) You will hear people talking in eight different situations. For questions **1–8**, choose the best answer, **A**, **B** or **C**.

1   You hear two teenagers talking about a lost scarf.
    Where does the girl think she lost it?
    A   on the bus
    B   in the street
    C   in a shop

2   You hear two people talking about a proposed new motorway.
    What is the man worried about?
    A   the noise from fast-moving traffic
    B   the loss of local sports facilities
    C   the permanent harm to the countryside

3   You hear a radio announcer giving a traffic update.
    Who is his advice for?
    A   People going shopping.
    B   People going to watch football.
    C   People going to a music festival.

4   You overhear a woman talking on the phone.
    What does she want the other person to do?
    A   to meet her somewhere
    B   to give someone else a message
    C   to buy something for her

5   You hear two people talking about holidays.
    What is the woman encouraging the man to do?
    A   visit particular countries
    B   go on an environmentally-friendly holiday
    C   travel with a large group of people

6   You hear an art critic talking about a famous painting.
    Why does he think it is so popular?
    A   It reflects a common human experience.
    B   It is worth an enormous amount of money.
    C   It is a particularly brilliant work of art.

7   You overhear a salesman talking about his job.
    How does he feel about it?
    A   keen to find work elsewhere
    B   worried that he might be replaced
    C   confident he will soon be promoted

8   You hear two people talking about a ferry ride to an island.
    What does the man say about the experience?
    A   He felt rather ill when he was on board.
    B   The ship had limited facilities for passengers.
    C   The crossing was no longer than he had expected.

(3) 06 You will hear a businesswoman called Jessica Morton talking on the radio about a car journey she made across a desert in Australia. For questions **9–18**, complete the sentences with a word or short phrase. **[You will need to play this recording twice.]**

Crossing the desert

Jessica says she had to be in the town of Alice Springs by Thursday for a **(9)** ....

Jessica discovered there was no train to Alice Springs on **(10)** .... in summer.

The village of Glendambo was Jessica's last chance to get petrol for **(11)** ....

When Jessica saw a **(12)** .... , she left the main road.

Jessica stopped the car when some **(13)** .... ran across in front of her.

Jessica tried putting some **(14)** .... under the wheels.

Jessica was shocked to find that her **(15)** .... didn't work in the desert.

Jessica stopped using the **(16)** .... when the sun went down.

When Jessica reached the building, she regretted leaving her **(17)** ....

Jessica found a way to get her own car moving when she looked at the **(18)** .... on another car.

[3] 07 You will hear five short extracts in which university students are talking about their next summer vacation. For questions **19–23**, choose from the list (**A–H**) what each speaker wants to do during their vacation. Use the letters only once. There are three extra letters which you do not need to use. [**You will need to play this recording twice.**]

___

A   start learning a language

B   spend time with friends

C   travel abroad

D   do charity work

E   read books

F   earn some money

G   learn to drive

H   do more exercise

Speaker 1 [   ] **19**

Speaker 2 [   ] **20**

Speaker 3 [   ] **21**

Speaker 4 [   ] **22**

Speaker 5 [   ] **23**

3 08 You will hear a radio interview with a woman called Amelia Richards, whose job involves planning people's weddings. For questions **24–30**, choose the best answer, **A**, **B** or **C**. **[You will need to play this recording twice.]**

24 Amelia says that a wedding planner is not responsible for

   A choosing the wedding dress.

   B discussing fees with the photographer.

   C advising on wedding customs.

25 Why, according to Amelia, do many couples employ a wedding planner?

   A They don't have enough time to plan it themselves.

   B Their families often can't agree on some of the details.

   C It is cheaper than if they try to organise it themselves.

26 Amelia decided to become a wedding planner following her experience of

   A working in the catering industry.

   B organising her own wedding.

   C helping to run charity events.

27 Amelia believes she is good at

   A selecting the best-paid wedding planning jobs.

   B planning more than one wedding at a time.

   C managing to remain calm under pressure.

28 How is Amelia paid?

   A She charges according to the number of hours she has worked.

   B She receives a percentage of the total cost of the wedding.

   C She gets a fixed fee for every kind of wedding.

29 What does Amelia dislike about her job?

   A She has little time each year to take holidays.

   B There is no guaranteed income from her work.

   C She often has to work evenings and weekends.

30 Amelia says the best way to get work as a wedding planner is to show people

   A pictures of events you have successfully organised.

   B references from people who have used your services.

   C your qualifications in wedding planning.

---

Part 1

2 minutes (3 minutes for groups of three)

Interlocutor First of all, we'd like to know something about you.

- Tell us about the best book you have ever read.
- What is your favourite place to read?
- Which sport or hobby would you like to take up? Why?
- Who is your favourite sportsperson? Why?
- Tell us how people in your country celebrate New Year.

4 minutes (6 minutes for groups of three)

Interlocutor In this part of the test, I'm going to give each of you two photographs. I'd like you to talk about your photographs on your own for about a minute, and also to answer a question about your partner's photographs.

(Candidate A), it's your turn first. Here are your photographs on page C18. They show **people listening to music while they do other things**.

I'd like you to compare the photographs, and say **why you think the people are listening to music**.

All right?

Candidate A ....

Interlocutor Thank you.

(Candidate B), **When and where do you listen to music?**

Candidate B ....

Interlocutor Thank you.

Now, *(Candidate B),* here are your photographs on page C19. They show **people working in television**.

I'd like you to compare the photographs, and say **how difficult you think each person's job might be**.

All right?

Candidate B ....

Interlocutor Thank you.

(Candidate A), **Which of these jobs would you prefer to do?**

Candidate A ....

Interlocutor Thank you.

Part 3   4 minutes (5 minutes for groups of three)

Interlocutor   Now, I'd like you to talk about something together for about two minutes. (3 minutes for groups of three)

I'd like you to imagine that a sports club wants to advertise to encourage more people to use its facilities.

First you have some time to look at the task.

Show candidates the diagram on page C20. Allow 15 seconds.

Now, talk to each other about **why these kinds of advertising would encourage more people to use the club.**

Allow two minutes (three minutes for groups of three).

Interlocutor   Thank you. Now you have a minute to decide **which of these kinds of advertising would be the most effective.**

Allow one minute for pairs or groups of three.

Thank you.

Part 4   4 minutes (6 minutes for groups of three)

Interlocutor Select any of the following questions, as appropriate.
- Some people say advertising encourages us to buy things we don't really need. What do you think?
- Is it more enjoyable to watch a TV programme with advertising breaks, or without them? (Why?)
- Do you think people are more likely to buy a product if a celebrity recommends it? (Why?/Why not?)
- Which is the best advertisement you have ever seen? Why was it so good?
- Should firms be allowed to advertise to children? (Why?/Why not?)
- In your country, which types of product are advertised the most? Why do you think that is?

Select any of the following prompts, as appropriate.

> - **What do you think?**
> - **Do you agree?**
> - **And you?**

Thank you. That is the end of the test.

Acknowledgements

Author acknowledgements

The authors and publishers acknowledge the following sources of copyright material and are grateful for the permissions granted. While every effort has been made, it has not always been possible to identify the sources of all the material used, or to trace all copyright holders. If any omissions are brought to our notice, we will be happy to include the appropriate acknowledgements on reprinting.

Amanda Martin for the text on pp. 25-26 adapted from *Two Hundred Steps Home* by Amanda Martin, published at http://www.amazon.co.uk/dp/B00HOG97PW. Reprinted by permission.;

The Independent for the text on p. 30 adapted from article 'The ultimate green home – down to the rainwater in the toilets: The WWF's new headquarters is no glasshouse' by Tom Peck, 1 November 2013, *The Independent* (www.independent.co.uk) Copyright © The Independent 2013. Reprinted by permission;

The Independent for the text on pp. 76-77 adapted from article 'A lot can happen in a year abroad' by Sarah Morrison, 17 August 2010, *The Independent* (www.independent.co.uk) Copyright © The Independent 2010. Reprinted by permission;

The Independent for the text on p. 78 adapted from article 'I want your job: TV news producer' by Tom Mendelsohn, 22 July 2013, *The Independent* (www.independent.co.uk) Copyright © The Independent 2013. Reprinted by permission;

Victoria Rollison for the text on p. 112 adapted from *Conspire*, published by Smashwords 2012. Reprinted by permission;

The Independent for the text on p. 114 adapted from article 'Sweden: Go with the floe this winter' by Duncan Craig, 23 November 2013, *The Independent* (www.independent.co.uk) Copyright © The Independent 2013. Reprinted by permission;

Guardian News & Media Ltd for the text on p. 131 adapted from article 'Daniel Radcliffe: 'There's no master plan to distance myself from Harry Potter'' by Simon Hattenstone, 23 November 2013, *The Guardian* © Guardian News and Media Ltd 2013. Reprinted by permission;

The Independent for the text on p. 133 adapted from article 'Driven to distraction: Have we lost the ability to focus on a single task?' by Archie Bland, 2 November 2013, *The Independent* (www.independent.co.uk) Copyright © The Independent 2013. Reprinted by permission;

Simon Collings for the text on p. 150 adapted from *Night Flight* by Simon Collings, first published on www.short-stories.co.uk. Reprinted by permission;

The Independent for the text on p. 152 adapted from article 'Just because I've been on holiday doesn't mean I have to be happy' by Rebecca Armstrong, 22 July 2013, *The Independent* (www.independent.co.uk) Copyright © The Independent 2013. Reprinted by permission;

Telegraph Media Group (TMG) for the text on p. 169 adapted from article 'Distance learning: study while you work' by Josie Gurney-Read, 21 October 2013 © Telegraph Media Group Limited 2012. Reprinted by permission;

The Independent for the text on p. 171 adapted from article 'Can we control our dreams?' by Dan Roberts, 21 June 2011, *The Independent* (www.independent.co.uk) Copyright © The Independent 2011. Reprinted by permission.

Photo acknowledgements

The authors and publishers acknowledge the following sources of copyright material and are grateful for the permissions granted. While every effort has been made, it has not always been possible to identify the sources of all the material used, or to trace all copyright holders. If any omissions are brought to our notice, we will be happy to include the appropriate acknowledgements on reprinting.

p. 25: Shutterstock/© iofoto; p. 28: Shutterstock/© Gabriele Maltinti; p. 30: Alamy/© dbphots; p. 33: Shutterstock/© Styve Reineck; p. 35: Shutterstock/© Permchai Phoorivatana; p. 44: Shutterstock/© muzsy; p. 45: Shutterstock/© JonMilnes; p. 50: Shutterstock/© Neamov; p. 53: Alamy/© vaver anton; p. 55: Alamy/© Blue Jean Images; p. 69: Shuttestock/© Fernando Jose V. Soares; p. 71: Alamy/© Photofusion Picture Library; p. 81: Alamy/© Albuquerque Journal/ ZUMAPRESS. Com; p. 83: Shutterstock/© TonyV3112; p. 84: Alamy/© A.P.S (UK); p. 86: Corbis/© Tomas Rodriguez; p. 87: Shutterstock/© oliveromg; p. 89: Shutterstock/© Plamen Peev; p. 90: Shutterstock/© Pavel L Photo and Video; p. 93: Shutterstock/© CREATISTA; p. 96: Shutterstock/© Jeffy11390; p. 109: Shutterstock/© Tupungato; p. 110: Alamy/© Robert Johns; p. 112: Shutterstock/© Martin Maun; p. 114: Alamy/© Westend61 GmbH; p. 116: Shutterstock/© Nanisimova; p. 118: Rex Features/© Encyclopaedia Britannica/UIG; p. 128: Alamy/© Richard G. Bingham II; p. 131 (T): Ronald Grant Archive/© Warner Bros/JK Rowling; p. 131 (B): Rex Features/© Broadimage; p. 133: Corbis/© JGI/Jamie Grill/Blend Images; p. 135: Getty Images/© E+/Izabela Habur; p. 137: Corbis/© 64/ Ocean; p. 140: Alamy/© Radius Images; p. 142: Alamy/© wareham. no (sport); p. 145: Shutterstock/© Steve Estvanik; p. 155: Getty Images/© Michael Steele; p. 156: Shutterstock/© oliveromg; p. 159: Shutterstock/© Markus Gann; p. 160: Corbis/© Mika; p. 161: Shutterstock/© imagedb.com; p. 169: Shutterstock/© Ulrich Willmunder; p. 173: Shutterstock/© Ljupco Smokovski; p. 175: Alamy/© Janine Wiedel Photolibrary; p. 178: Alamy/© Bella Flak; p. 180: Alamy/© Don Tonge. C1 (T): Shutterstock/© wavebreakmedia; C1 (B): Shutterstock/© bikeriderlondon; C2 (T): Getty Images/© The Image Bank/White Packert; C2 (B): Alamy/© Blend Images; C3 (T): Thinkstock/© iStock/IPGGutenbergUKLtd; C3 (B): Alamy/© Terry Harris; C4 (T): Thinkstock/© Photodisc/Jack Hollingsworth; C4 (B): Shutterstock/© Fotoluminate LLC; C6 (T): Shutterstock/© wavebreakmedia; C6 (B): Alamy/© Chris Rout; C7 (T): Getty Images/© First Light/Kurt Werby; C7 (B): Alamy/© fraser band; C9 (T): Shutterstock/© michaeljung; C9 (B): Getty Images/© Cultura/Henglein and Steets; C10 (T): Alamy/© Chris Howes/Wild Places Photography; C10 (B): Getty Images/© The Image Bank/Ricky John Molloy; C12 (T): Superstock/© Yuri Arcurs Media; C12 (B): Shutterstock/© Syda Productions; C13 (T): Corbis/© Tim Clayton; C13 (B): Alamy/© Alex Sagre; C15 (T): Thinkstock/© Photos.com/ Hemera Technologies; C15 (B): Getty Images/© The RFU Collection/ David Rogers; C16 (T): Alamy/© Peter E Noyce; C16 (B): Getty Images/© LOOK/Franz Marc Frei; C18 (T): Corbis/© Jose Luis Pelaez/Blend Images; C18 (B): Corbis/© 2/Ocean; C19: Rex Features/© Sipa Press.

Illustrations by:

Mike Lacey (Beehive Illustration) pp. 11, 37, 40, 46, 49, 57, 121, 122, 150, 152, 164; Dan Lewis (Beehive Illustration) pp.13, 18, 73, 75, 129, 148

Design, layout and art edited by: Wild Apple Design Ltd.

A

B

- Why are the two different kinds of relationship important to teenagers?

A

B

• Why do you think people choose to shop in these different places?

A

B

- How important do you think the relationship is to the different people?

A

B

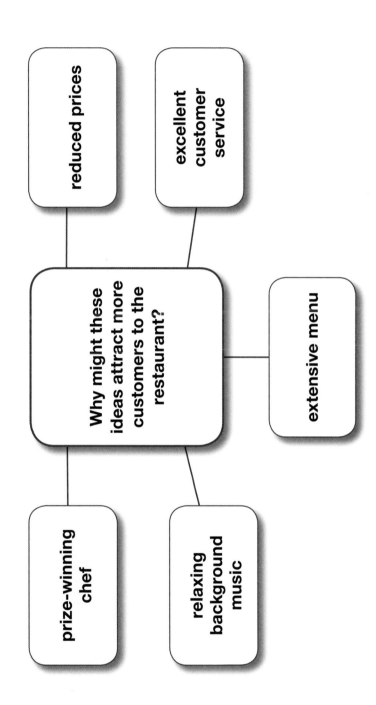

reduced prices

excellent customer service

Why might these ideas attract more customers to the restaurant?

extensive menu

prize-winning chef

relaxing background music

- Why do you think the people are writing?

A

B

- How might the snow affect the different people?

C

D

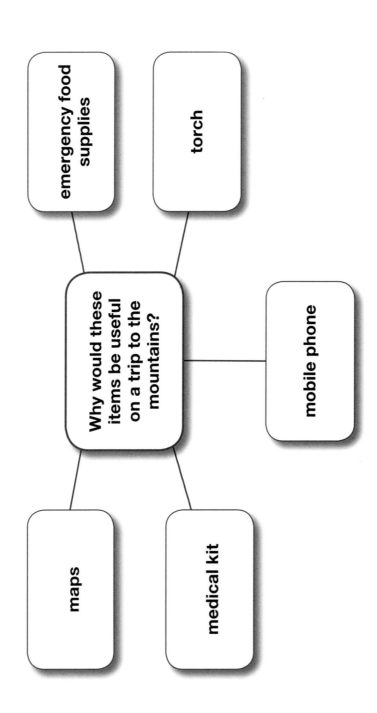

Why would these items be useful on a trip to the mountains?

- emergency food supplies
- torch
- mobile phone
- maps
- medical kit

- **What do you think the people are enjoying about the occasions?**

> • How do you think the people in each queue are feeling?

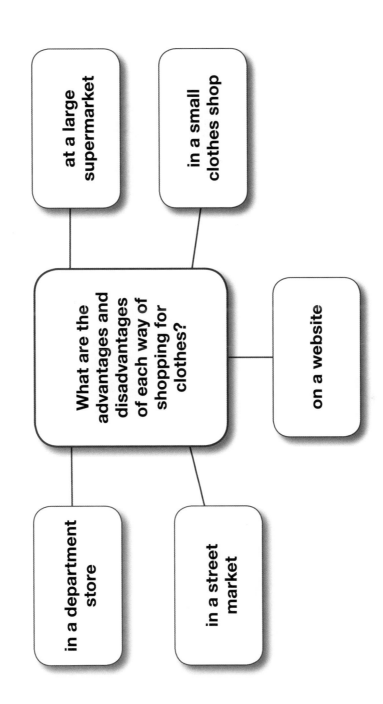

at a large supermarket

in a small clothes shop

What are the advantages and disadvantages of each way of shopping for clothes?

on a website

in a department store

in a street market

> • How do you think the people in the photographs probably feel?

- What are the different people enjoying about being in these parks?

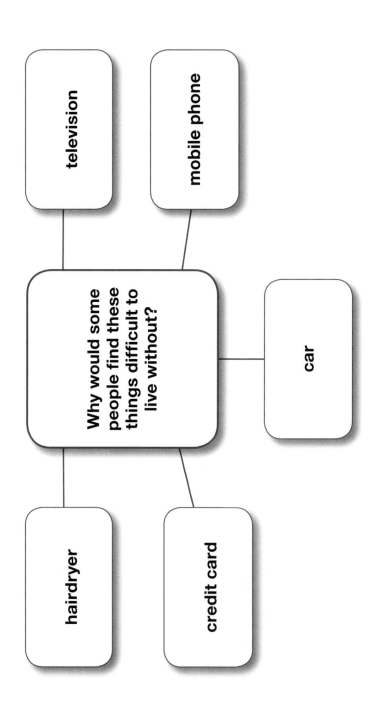

television

mobile phone

Why would some people find these things difficult to live without?

car

hairdryer

credit card

- Why are the people singing in these different places?

- What do you think the people find interesting about the two different kinds of art?

C

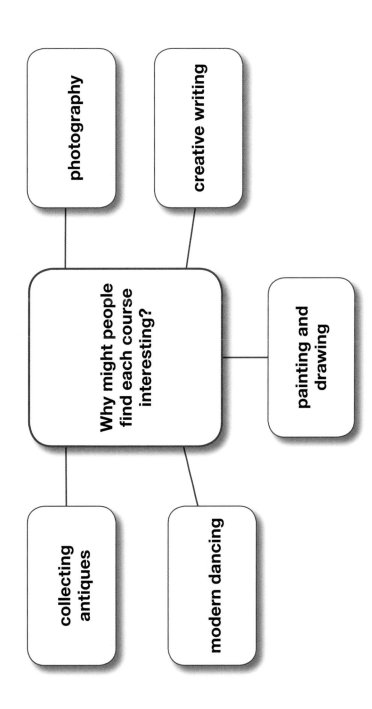

photography

creative writing

Why might people find each course interesting?

painting and drawing

collecting antiques

modern dancing

• Why do you think the people are listening to music?

> • How difficult do you think each person's job might be?

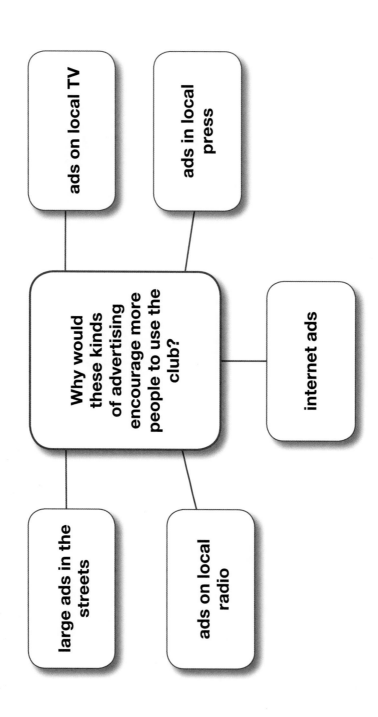

ads on local TV

ads in local press

internet ads

Why would these kinds of advertising encourage more people to use the club?

large ads in the streets

ads on local radio